Knits

FOR YOU AND YOUR HOME

Photography by Penny Wincer

Quadrille
PUBLISHING

Knits

FOR YOU AND YOUR HOME

Debbie Bliss

Contents

Introduction 6 ✳ Types of Yarn 8 ✳ Standard Abbreviations 11

PAMPER 12
✳ Bath Bag 14 ✳ Lavender Hearts 18 ✳ Cape Coat 22
✳ Storage Jar Bands 28 ✳ Sleep Mask 32 ✳ Pouffe 36
✳ Heated Neck Pillow 40

COCOON 44
✳ Armchair Throw 46 ✳ Trapper Hat 50 ✳ Slippers 54
✳ Slouchy Hat 58 ✳ Chair Back 62 ✳ Snood 66
✳ Cabled Socks 70 ✳ Waterfall Jacket 74

DETOX 80
✳ Accessories Holder 82 ✳ Message Board 86
✳ Double Moss Stitch Tunic 90 ✳ Storage File 96
✳ Wine Bottle Covers 100 ✳ Magazine Holder 106
✳ Extra Wide Cardigan 110 ✳ Hanging Pockets 116

INDULGE 120
✳ Beaded Cushion 122 ✳ Watchstraps 126 ✳ Shrug 130
✳ Keepsake Box 136 ✳ Headband 140 ✳ Lace Collar 144
✳ Chevron Cushion 148 ✳ Lacy Shawl 152

Yarn Distributors 156 ✳ Acknowledgements 160

In a world in which we are all perpetually 'on the go' and under a constant pressure to be everything to everyone, the day-to-day stresses of life can make it difficult to carve out time for ourselves.

Whenever I meet knitters I am reminded time and time again that they are some of the most selfless of people; so many times I hear the refrain 'I am making this project for a friend/partner/grandchild' or the classic phrase 'I never have time to make anything for myself.' So with this book of over thirty designs I hope to entice the crafter – if only for a short time – away from the projects they are planning to make for everyone else and to knit something for themselves. (Although should it be admired, of course, there is no reason why it can't join the list of knits to make for others!)

I have divided the book into four sections – Pamper, Cocoon, Detox and Indulge – and each contains a mix of knits to wear as well as projects to help decorate and organise your home.

Pamper is for the ultimate time out, so bring the spa into your home and put your feet up on a giant pouffe, drift off with a sleep mask or make hearts containing relaxing lavender. While for those of you who like me suffer from 'knitter's neck' there is a neck cushion that can be heated up for extra soothing powers.

Cocoon has knits to envelop and comfort you, from super-soft throws and a snuggly snood to cosy chair covers. The designs to wear are in luxurious fibres, which are ever so gentle against your skin.

Detox is for those who sometimes relax by pottering around. I relax by sorting out my crayons by colour or my sketchbooks by size, rearranging my mood boards, gently tidying (but nothing too energetic!), so in this section I have included projects that will help you to sort, stack and tuck away.

Indulge has projects to make you feel that little bit extra-special, bringing some well-deserved glamour into your life. Get some movie-queen style with delicate knits in super-fine, gossamer-like mohair, a 1920s-style turban for your inner flapper and a beautiful classic beaded purse.

Many of the projects are quick to make or use only a single ball, so go on, take some time out for yourself – you are worth it.

This book would not have been possible without the invaluable help of Rosy Tucker who came up with the wonderful home makes while I concentrated on the wearables. We hope you enjoy the book.

Debbie Bliss

Types of yarn

The yarns I have chosen for the designs in this book range from my organic cotton to cashmerinos and pure wools, each with their own unique qualities that contribute to the designs. It may be that they give crisp stitch detail in a simple pattern, such as the accessories holder (right and page 82) worked in cotton, or provide softness and elegance in a garment, such as the shrug (page 130) knitted in a mohair/silk blend.

Unless you are using up your stash to make the smaller items in this book, make the effort to buy the yarn stated in the pattern. Each of these designs has been created with a specific yarn in mind.

A different yarn may not produce the same quality of fabric or have the same wash and wear properties. From an aesthetic point of view, the clarity of a subtle stitch pattern may be lost if a project is knitted in an inferior yarn. However, there may be occasions when a knitter needs to substitute a yarn – if there is an allergy to wool, for example – and so the following is a guide to making the most informed choices.

Always buy a yarn that is the same weight as that given in the pattern: replace a double knitting with a double knitting, for example, and check that the tension of both yarns is the same.

Where you are substituting a different fibre, be aware of the design. A cable pattern knitted in cotton when worked in wool will pull in because of the greater elasticity of the yarn and so the fabric will become narrower; this will alter the proportions of the knitting.

Check the metreage of the yarn. Yarns that weigh the same may have different lengths in the ball or hank, so you may need to buy more or less yarn.

The following are descriptions of my yarns used in this book and a guide to their weights and types (see page 10).

Debbie Bliss Andes:
* A double-knitting-weight yarn.
* 65% baby alpaca, 35% mulberry silk.
* Approximately 100m/50g hank.

Debbie Bliss Angel:
* A lightweight mohair-blend yarn.
* 76% superkid mohair, 24% silk.
* Approximately 200m/25g ball.

Debbie Bliss Baby Cashmerino:
* A lightweight yarn between a 4ply and a DK.
* 55% merino wool, 33% microfibre, 12% cashmere.
* Approximately 125m/50g ball.

Debbie Bliss Cashmerino Aran:
* An aran-weight yarn.
* 55% merino wool, 33% microfibre, 12% cashmere.
* Approximately 90m/50g ball.

Debbie Bliss Cashmerino DK:
* A double-knitting-weight yarn.
* 55% merino wool, 33% microfibre, 12% cashmere.
* Approximately 110m/50g ball.

Debbie Bliss Cotton DK:
* A double-knitting-weight yarn.
* 100% cotton.
* Approximately 84m/50g ball.

Debbie Bliss Eco Baby:
* A lightweight yarn between a 4ply and a DK.
* 100% organic cotton.
* Approximately 125m/50g ball.

Debbie Bliss Paloma:
* A chunky-weight yarn.
* 60% baby alpaca, 40% merino wool.
* Approximately 65m/50g ball.

Debbie Bliss Party Angel:
* A lightweight mohair-blend yarn.
* 72% superkid mohair, 24% silk, 4% metallized polyester.
* Approximately 200m/25g ball.

Debbie Bliss Rialto Aran:
* An aran-weight yarn.
* 100% extra fine merino wool.
* Approximately 80m/50g ball.

Debbie Bliss Rialto Chunky:
* A chunky-weight yarn.
* 100% merino wool.
* Approximately 60m/50g ball.

Debbie Bliss Rialto 4ply:
* A 4ply-weight yarn.
* 100% extra fine merino wool.
* Approximately 180m/50g ball.

Debbie Bliss Rialto Lace:
* A lace-weight yarn.
* 100% extra fine merino wool.
* Approximately 390m/50g ball.

Buying yarn

The ball band on the yarn will carry all the essential information you need as to tension, needle size, weight and yardage. Importantly it will also have the dye lot. Yarns are dyed in batches or lots, which can vary considerably. Your retailer may not have the same dye lot later on, so buy all your yarn for a project at the same time. If you know that sometimes you use more yarn than that quoted in the pattern, buy extra. If it is not possible to buy all the yarn you need with the same dye lot, use the different ones where it will not show as much, on a neck or border, as a change of dye lot across a main piece will be more visible.

At the time of buying the yarn, check the pattern and make sure you already have the needles you require. If not, buy them now, as it will save a lot of frustration when you get home.

Abbreviations

In a book common abbreviations are given at the front before the patterns begin, whilst any more specific to a particular design are given at the start of the individual pattern. The abbreviations on the facing page are used throughout this book.

STANDARD ABBREVIATIONS

alt	alternate
beg	begin(ning)
cont	continue
dec	decrease(ing)
foll	following
inc	increase(ing)
k	knit
kfb	knit into front and back of next stitch
m1	make one stitch by picking up the loop lying between the stitch just worked and the next stitch and working into the back of it
p	purl
patt	pattern
psso	pass slipped stitch over
rem	remain(ing)
rep	repeat(ing)
skpo	slip 1, knit 1, pass slipped stitch over
sl	slip
ssk	[slip 1 knitwise] twice, insert tip of left-hand needle from left to right through fronts of slipped stitches and k2tog
st(s)	stitch(es)
st st	stocking stitch
tbl	through back loop
tog	together
yf	yarn forward
yo or **yon**	yarn over needle
yrn	yarn round needle

Pamper

Bath Bag

This bag is perfect for keeping all your bathroom accessories in. Hang on the back of your bathroom door to ensure it is always to hand and fill with all your special pampering products. No longer will you have to scrabble around trying to find your bathroom treats, you can feel organised and relaxed. Knitted in a classic combination of ecru and stone and lined with an attractive spotty fabric, this easily transportable bath bag will suit every bathroom.

SIZE
Approximately 63cm (25¼in) in circumference x 28cm (11in) tall from base

MATERIALS
* 6 x 50g balls of Debbie Bliss Cotton DK in ecru (A) and 4 x 50g balls in stone (B)
* Pair of 5.50mm (US 9) knitting needles
* 27 x 15cm (10¾ x 6in) piece of cardboard
* 32cm (12½in) of 90cm (36in) wide lining fabric
* Sewing thread

TENSION
16 sts and 24 rows to 10cm (4in) square over patt using 5.50mm (US 9) needles and two strands of yarn used together.

ABBREVIATIONS
pkp [purl, knit, purl] all into next st. Also see page 11.

NOTE

The bag is made in one piece.

TO MAKE

Bag base

With 5.50mm (US 9) needles and two strands of B used together, cast on 29 sts.

1st row (right side) K1, [p1, k1] to end.

2nd row K1, pkp, [k1, p1] 5 times, k1, [pkp, k1] twice, [p1, k1] 5 times, pkp, k1. **37 sts.**

3rd row As 1st row.

4th row [K1, pkp] twice, [k1, p1] 5 times, k1, [pkp, k1] 4 times, [p1, k1] 5 times, [pkp, k1] twice. **53 sts.**

5th row As 1st row.

6th row [K1, pkp] twice, [k1, p1] 9 times, k1, [pkp, k1] 4 times, [p1, k1] 9 times, [pkp, k1] twice. **69 sts.**

7th and 8th rows As 1st row.

9th row [K1, pkp] twice, [k1, p1] 13 times, k1, [pkp, k1] 4 times, [p1, k1] 13 times, [pkp, k1] twice. **85 sts.**

10th, 11th and 12th rows As 1st row.

13th row [K1, pkp] twice, [k1, p1] 17 times, k1, [pkp, k1] 4 times, [p1, k1] 17 times, [pkp, k1] twice. **101 sts.**

14th and 15th rows As 1st row.

1st ridge row (wrong side) K all sts.

2nd ridge row (right side) P all sts.

Main bag

Change to two strands of A used together and work in patt as follows:

1st row (wrong side) Purl.

2nd row P2, [k1, p3] to last 3 sts, k1, p2.

3rd row Purl.

4th row K1, [p3, k1] to end.

These 4 rows **form** the main patt and are repeated until work measures 25cm (10in) from 2nd ridge row, ending with a 2nd or 4th row.

Change to two strands of B used together and beg with a p row, cont in patt for a further 6 rows.

Cast off knitwise on wrong side.

STRAPS (make 2)

With 5.50mm (US 9) needles and two strands of B used together, cast on 5 sts.

Moss st row K1, [p1, k1] twice.

Rep last row until strap measures approximately 46cm (18in). Cast off in moss st.

TO MAKE UP

Fold cast on edge in half and join base seam to ridge rows, then continue to join the side seam to cast off edge.

Lining

Cut a cardboard oval shape for the base, approximately 15 x 27cm (6 x 10¾in). Use the cardboard shape to cut a base from lining, adding 1.5cm (⅝in) all round for seams. Cut a fabric rectangle approximately 32 x 74cm (12½ x 29¼in), then with right sides together, join the short ends together to form a tube, taking a 1cm (½in) seam. Stitch the lining base into the tube. Position the straps equally spaced on each side of the bag and stitch in place to the outside of the bag. Place the cardboard base into the bag, then slipstitch the lining into the bag around the top edge, turning the excess fabric onto the wrong side and matching the seam in the lining to the seam in the bag.

Lavender Hearts

These pretty and delicious smelling hanging hearts take just a single ball of Baby Cashmerino to make a set of three, plus some inexpensive silver embroidery beads for added sparkle. Although the beading makes these hearts look complicated, they are in fact deceptively simple to make as each bead is threaded onto the yarn before being worked into the knitted fabric. The patterned backing fabric takes this sophisticated design a step further by allowing you to add your own personality to each heart.

SIZE
Approximately 9 x 9cm (3$\frac{1}{2}$ x 3$\frac{1}{2}$in)

MATERIALS
✷ 1 x 50g ball of Debbie Bliss Baby Cashmerino in silver
✷ Pair of 3.25mm (US 3) knitting needles
✷ 82 glass embroidery beads per heart – silver-lined clear glass beads, size SB07 colour 1 (www.creativebeadcraft.co.uk)
✷ 13cm (5in) square piece of fabric for each heart
✷ Lengths of 3mm (⅛in) wide ribbon
✷ Dried lavender flowers
✷ Optional lavender essential oil to enhance the aroma or freshen old lavender

TENSION
25 sts and 34 rows to 10cm (4in) square over st st using 3.25mm (US 3) needles.

ABBREVIATIONS
PB bring yarn to front of work, slip 1 st, push bead along the yarn close to the work, take the yarn to back of work. Also see page 11.

BEADING NOTE

* Before casting on, you need to thread the beads onto the yarn. If your beading needle is made from very fine gauge wire with a long collapsible eye, you can thread the beads directly onto the yarn. If you have to use a fine needle with a small eye, you need to thread the needle with a length of sewing thread tied to form a loop, then thread the yarn through the loop, so the beads thread onto the sewing thread first, then onto the yarn.

* The beads need to have a centre hole large enough for two thicknesses of yarn to pass through, or you will not be able to thread the beads. You may find a few beads that have a slightly smaller centre hole, this is due to a thicker than normal coating of silver. You will need to discard these but one 15g tube of beads should be sufficient for 3 hearts.

TO MAKE

With 3.25mm (US 3) needles, cast on 3 sts.
1st and every foll wrong side row Purl.
2nd row K1, [m1, k1] twice. 5 sts.
4th row K1, m1, k1, p1, k1, m1, k1. 7 sts.
6th row K1, m1, k2, PB, k2, m1, k1. 9 sts.
8th row K1, m1, k1, PB, k3, B1, k1, m1, k1. 11 sts.
10th row K1, m1, PB, [k3, PB] twice, m1, k1. 13 sts.
12th row K1, m1, k3, [PB, k3] twice, m1, k1. 15 sts.
14th row K1, m1, k2, [PB, k3] twice, PB, k2, m1, k1. 17 sts.
16th row K1, m1, k1, [PB, k3] 3 times, PB, k1, m1, k1. 19 sts.
18th row K1, m1, [PB, k3] 4 times, PB, m1, k1. 21 sts.
20th row K4, [PB, k3] 4 times, k1.
22nd row K1, m1, k1, [PB, k3] 4 times, PB, k1, m1, k1. 23 sts.
24th row K1, [PB, k3] 5 times, PB, k1.
26th row K1, m1, k2, [PB, k3] 4 times, PB, k2, m1, k1. 25 sts.
28th row K2, [PB, k3] 5 times, PB, k2.
30th row K1, m1, k3, [PB, k3] 5 times, m1, k1. 27 sts.
32nd row K3, [PB, k3] 6 times.
34th row K1, [PB, k3] 6 times, PB, k1.
36th row K3, [PB, k3] 6 times.
37th row P to end.

Shape top of first side

38th row (right side) K1, [PB, k3] 3 times, turn and leave rem 14 sts on a holder.
39th row P2tog, p to end. 12 sts.
40th row K2tog tbl, k1, [PB, k3] twice, k1. 11 sts.
41st row P2tog, p to end. 10 sts.
42nd row K2tog tbl, k2, PB, k5. 9 sts.
43rd row P2tog, p to last 2 sts, p2tog tbl. 8 sts.
44th row K2tog tbl, k4, k2tog. 6 sts.
Cast off row P2tog, [p1, pass 1st st over 2nd st] twice, p2tog tbl, pass 1st st over 2nd st, fasten off last st.

Shape top of second side

38th row With right side facing, join yarn to rem 14 sts on holder, k2tog tbl, k2, [PB, k3] twice, PB, k1. 13 sts.
39th row P1, p to last 2 sts, p2tog tbl. 12 sts.
40th row K4, PB, k3, PB, k1, k2tog. 11 sts.
41st row P to last 2 sts, p2tog tbl. 10 sts.
42nd row K5, PB, k2, k2tog. 9 sts.
43rd row P to last 2 sts, p2tog tbl. 8 sts.
44th row K2tog tbl, k4, k2tog. 6 sts.
Cast off row P2tog, [p1, pass 1st st over 2nd st] twice, p2tog tbl, pass 1st st over 2nd st and fasten off.

TO MAKE UP

Using the knitted heart as a template, cut a piece of fabric to shape, adding 5mm (3/8in) all around the edge. Lay knitted heart onto fabric heart with right sides together and carefully stitch around the edge, leaving a gap along one side to turn through. Clip the fabric around the curved edges and turn through to right side. Cut a length of ribbon and tie the two ends together securely and find the centre (opposite the knot). Thread the ribbon into a large eyed needle and working through the gap in the seam, thread the needle with the ribbon through the V of the heart, so forming a hanging loop with the knot holding it in place inside the heart. Fold the seam allowance along the gap onto the wrong side, fill the heart with lavender and sew the gap closed.

Cape Coat

This luxury coat is perfect for all occasions – whether you wear it whilst lounging around your home, taking your children to school, meeting friends or even doing all three, you will feel comfortable and look stylish. I have made this warming coat in a neutral beige to ensure it goes with every outfit and eventuality, but if you prefer, make it a statement piece by knitting it in a more striking colour. This classically designed simple cape coat will look wonderful in any shade.

MEASUREMENTS

To fit bust

81–86	92–97	102–107	cm
32–34	36–38	40–42	in

Finished measurements

Width

100	111	123	cm
39½	43¾	48½	in

Length to shoulder

77	80	84	cm
30¼	31½	33	in

MATERIALS

- 20(22:24) x 50g balls of Debbie Bliss Cashmerino DK in beige
- One 4mm (US 6) circular knitting needle
- Pair of 3.25mm (US 3) knitting needles
- One large button

TENSION

26 sts and 30 rows to 10cm (4in) square over patt using 4mm (US 6) needles.

ABBREVIATIONS

See page 11.

BACK

With 4mm (US 6) circular needle, cast on 210 (234:258) sts.

Work backwards and forwards in rows.

1st row (right side) P2, [k2, p2] to end.

2nd row K2, [p2, k2] to end.

These 2 rows **form** the rib and are repeated.

Rib 3 more rows.

Inc row (wrong side) K2, [p1, m1, p1, k2] to end. **262 (292:322) sts.**

Now work in patt as follows:

1st row P2, [sl 1, k2, psso, p2] to end.

2nd row K2, [p1, yrn, p1, k2] to end.

3rd row P2, [k3, p2] to end.

4th row K2, [p3, k2] to end.

These 4 rows **form** the patt and are repeated.

Cont in patt until back measures 51 (52:53)cm/ 20 (20½:21)in from cast on edge, ending with a wrong side row.

Shape upper arms

Cast off 2 sts at beg of next 78 (86:94) rows. **106 (120:134) sts.**

Shape shoulders

Cast off 11 (13:15) sts at beg of next 4 rows and 11 (12:13) sts at beg of foll 2 rows. **40 (44:48) sts.**

Cast off.

LEFT FRONT

With 4mm (US 6) circular needle, cast on 112 (124:136) sts.

Work backwards and forwards in rows.

1st row (right side) [P2, k2] to last 8 sts, k8.

2nd row K8, [p2, k2] to end.

These 2 rows **form** the rib with garter st front edge and are repeated.

Work a further 3 rows.

Inc row (wrong side) K8, [p1, m1, p1, k2] to end. **138 (153:168) sts.**

Now work in patt as follows:

1st row [P2, sl 1, k2, psso] to last 8 sts, k8.

2nd row K8, [p1, yrn, p1, k2] to end.

3rd row [P2, k3] to last 8 sts, k8.

4th row K8, [p3, k2] to end.

These 4 rows **form** the patt with garter st front edge and are repeated.

Cont in patt until front measures 51 (52:53)cm/ 20 (20½:21)in from cast on edge, ending with a wrong side row.

Shape upper arm

Cast off 2 sts at beg of next row and 29 (33:37) foll right side rows. **78 (85:92) sts.**

Next row Patt to end.

Shape neck

Next row Cast off 2 sts, patt to last 11 (13:15) sts, leave these 11 (13:15) sts on a holder, turn and work on rem sts. **65 (70:75) sts.**

Next row Cast off 2 sts, patt to end.

Next row Cast off 2 sts, patt to end.

Rep the last 2 rows 7 times more.

Next row Patt to end. **33 (38:43) sts.**

Shape shoulder

Cast off 11 (13:15) sts at beg of next row and foll right side row.

Work 1 row.

Cast off rem 11 (12:13) sts.

RIGHT FRONT

With 4mm (US 6) circular needle, cast on 112(124:136) sts.

Work backwards and forwards in rows.

1st row (right side) K8, [k2, p2] to end.

2nd row [K2, p2] to last 8 sts, k8.

These 2 rows **form** the rib with garter st front edge and are repeated.

Work a further 3 rows.

Inc row [K2, p1, m1, p1] to last 8 sts, k8. **138(153:168) sts.**

Now work in patt as follows:

1st row K8, [sl 1, k2, psso, p2] to end.

2nd row [K2, p1, yrn, p1] to last 8 sts, k8.

3rd row K8, [k3, p2] to end.

4th row [K2, p3] to last 8 sts, k8.

These 4 rows **form** the patt with garter st edge and are repeated.

Cont in patt until front measures 51(52:53)cm/20(20½:21)in from cast on edge, ending with a right side row.

Shape upper arm

Cast off 2 sts at beg of next row and 30(34:38) foll wrong side rows. **76(83:90) sts.**

Shape neck

Next row Patt 11(13:15) sts, leave these 11(13:15) sts on a holder, patt to end. **65(70:75) sts**

Next row Cast off 2 sts, patt to end.

Next row Cast off 2 sts, patt to end.

Rep the last 2 rows 7 times more. **33(38:43) sts.**

Shape shoulder

Cast off 11(13:15) sts at beg of next row and foll right side row.

Work 1 row.

Cast off rem 11(12:13) sts.

NECKBAND

Join shoulder and upper arm seams.

With 3.25mm (US 3) needles, slip 11(13:15) sts from right front holder onto a needle, pick up and k22 sts up right front neck, 40(44:48) sts from back neck, 22 sts down left front neck, then patt 11(13:15) sts from left front holder. **106(114:122) sts.**

K 5 rows.

Buttonhole row K4, k2tog, y2rn, skpo, k to end.

Next row K to end, working k1, k1 tbl into y2rn.

K 8 rows.

Cast off.

ARMBANDS

Mark a point 20(21:22)cm/8(8¼:8¾)in down from upper arm seam on back and front.

With 3.25mm (US 3) needles, pick up and k79(83:87) sts between markers.

K 2 rows.

Cast off knitwise on wrong side.

TO MAKE UP

Join side and armband seams. Sew on button.

Back & Fronts

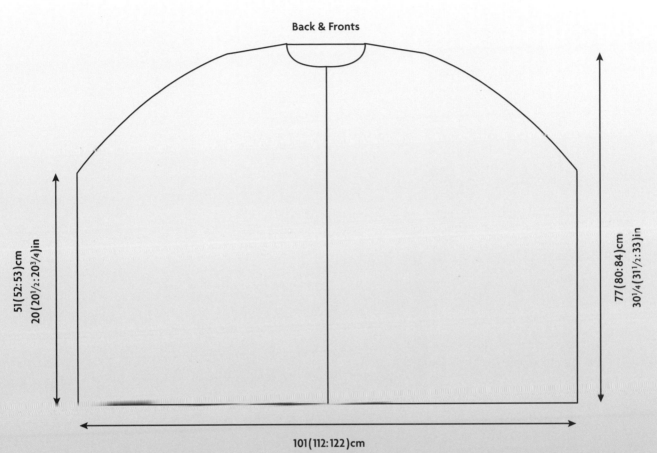

51(52:53)cm
20(20½:20¾)in

77(80:84)cm
30¼(31½:33)in

101(112:122)cm
39¾(44:48)in

Storage Jar Bands

This dainty pattern is a wonderful method for using up any remnants of wool that you may have lying around the house. These little bands will transform all your storage jars, turning something practical and often cluttered into an attractive and sophisticated item. These bands can be adapted to fit any size jar and as they are a small make that requires minimum time and effort to complete you will soon find that they become a necessity throughout all the rooms in your home.

SIZES
To fit jars with a diameter of 10cm (4in) and heights of 10cm (4in) and 16cm (6¼in) (see Notes)

MATERIALS
* 1 x 50g ball of Debbie Bliss Rialto 4ply in silver
* Pair of 2.75mm (US 2) knitting needles

TENSION
31.5 sts and 44 rows to 10cm (4in) square over patt using 2.75mm (US 2) needles.

ABBREVIATIONS
See page 11.

NOTES

The pattern is worked over a multiple of 9 sts plus an
extra 4 sts.
We used small and medium glass storage jars from
The White Company (www.thewhitecompany.com),
if you are using different sized jars, you will need to
adjust the number of stitches.

TO MAKE

The band is worked from the top down.
With 2.75mm (US 2) needles, cast on 94 sts.
1st row (wrong side) Purl.
2nd row K3, [yf, k2, skpo, k2tog, k2, yf, k1] 10 times, k1.
3rd row Purl.
4th row K2, [yf, k2, skpo, k2tog, k2, yf, k1] 10 times, k2.
These 4 rows **form** the patt and are repeated throughout.
Work in patt until piece measures 4cm (1½in) for short jar
or 9cm (3½in) for taller jar, ending with a right side row.
Cast off knitwise.

TO FINISH

Join row ends. Slip over the jars, with the straight cast off
edge at the base.

Sleep Mask

Nothing quite beats the restorative powers of a deep slumber, but in these hectic times it is often difficult to shut out the outside world. This cashmere and wool blend mask with a velour edging will help to lull you off to sleep, taking you to your own private dreamland. Using less than one ball of yarn, this sleep mask can easily be made in just a few hours, so if you start it in the afternoon you could be counting woolly sheep by bedtime.

SIZE
Approximately 7 x 18cm (2 3/4 x 7in)

MATERIALS
* 1 x 50g ball of Debbie Bliss Baby Cashmerino in light blue
* Pair of 3.25mm (US 3) knitting needles
* 10 x 20cm (4 x 8in) piece of cotton fabric for lining and same of thin wadding
* 0.5m (1/2yd) of 15mm (5/8in) wide soft elastic
* 0.5m (1/2yd) of enclosed velvet insertion braid 6004 (www.macculloch-wallis.co.uk)
* Sewing needle and thread to match lining fabric

TENSION
25 sts and 34 rows to 10cm (4in) square over patt using 3.25mm (US 3) needles.

ABBREVIATIONS
See page 11.

TO MAKE

With 3.25mm (US 3) needles, cast on 12 sts.

1st and every foll wrong side row (wrong side) P to end.

2nd row K1, m1, [p1, k3] twice, p1, k1, m1, k1. **14 sts.**

4th row K1, m1, [k3, p1] 3 times, m1, k1. **16 sts.**

6th row K1, m1, k2, [p1, k3] 3 times, m1, k1. **18 sts.**

8th row K1, m1, k1, [p1, k3] 4 times. **19 sts.**

10th row K1, [p1, k3] 4 times, p1, k1.

11th row P to end.

12th row K3, [p1, k3] 4 times.

13th row P to end.

10th to 13th rows **set** the patt and are repeated once more.

Now, keeping patt correct, dec 1 st at beg of next 8 right side rows, working the decs as k2tog tbl. **11 sts.**

Patt 7 rows straight, so ending with a p row.

Now, keeping patt correct, inc 1 st at beg of next 8 right side rows, working the incs as k1, m1. **19 sts.**

Patt 9 rows straight, so ending with a p row.

Next row (right side) K2tog tbl, k1, [p1, k3] 4 times. **18 sts.**

P 1 row.

Next row K2tog tbl, k2, [p1, k3] 3 times, k2tog. **16 sts.**

P 1 row.

Next row K2tog tbl, [k3, p1] 3 times, k2tog. **14 sts.**

P 1 row.

Next row K2tog tbl, [p1, k3] twice, p1, k1, k2tog. **12 sts.**

Cast off all sts knitwise.

TO MAKE UP

Using the knitted piece as a template, cut a paper shape. Cut a piece of wadding the same size and a piece of fabric adding a 5mm (¼in) seam allowance all around. Lay the wadding on the fabric and folding the seam allowance over the wadding, tack in place, close to the edge, you will need to clip the seam allowance where necessary. Sew one end of the elastic in place to the wrong side of the wadded fabric (mask lining), then allow approximately 36cm (14¼in) of elastic free before sewing the other end to the opposite side of the mask. Sew velvet piping to the edge of the mask lining. Lay the knitted piece onto the wrong side of the mask lining and easing to fit, sew close to the edge of the piping.

Pouffe

This soft knitted pouffe provides the perfect spot for some langorous lounging. Worked in moss stitch, the pouffe is made using three strands of cotton yarn held together to create a luxurious, oversized stitch. If you are unfamiliar with knitting on such a large scale, then make sure you practise first and do not skip the tension swatch stage. Also, when joining in new balls of yarn, do not add all three new strands at once but try to stagger them so that the joins are as imperceptible as possible.

SIZE
Approximately 38cm (15in) tall x 173cm (68in) all around

MATERIALS
* 21 x 50g balls of Debbie Bliss Cotton DK in duck egg
* Pair of long 9mm (US 13) knitting needles or one 9mm (US 13) circular knitting needle
* One kingsize machine washable polyester duvet

TENSION
11 sts and 17 rows to 10cm (4in) square over moss st using 9mm (US 13) needles and three strands of yarn held and used together.

ABBREVIATIONS
See page 11.

NOTES

If using a circular needle, work backwards and forwards in rows; do not work in rounds.

The piece is worked in turning rows throughout.

Do not wrap the sts when turning, but when slipping the st after turning, pull yarn tight to avoid a hole forming.

The pouffe will stretch once it is filled, so the recommended tension does not reflect the finished size.

TO MAKE

With 9mm (US 13) needles or circular needle and three strands of yarn used together, cast on 67 sts.

Moss st row K1, [p1, k1] to end.

This row **forms** moss st and is repeated.

Moss st one more row.

1st row (right side) Moss st to last 9 sts, turn.

2nd row Sl 1 purlwise pulling yarn tight (see Note), moss st to last 9 sts, turn.

3rd row Sl 1 purlwise, moss st last 3 sts, turn.

4th row Sl 1 purlwise, moss st to last 3 sts, turn.

5th row Sl 1 purlwise, moss st to last 9 sts, turn.

6th row Sl 1 purlwise, moss st to last 9 sts, turn.

7th row Sl 1 purlwise, moss st to last 15 sts, turn.

8th row Sl 1 purlwise, moss st to last 15 sts, turn.

9th row Sl 1 purlwise, moss st to end.

10th row Moss st across all sts. **

These 10 rows **form** the patt and are repeated 21 times more, then work 1st to 9th rows again.

Cast off all sts in moss st.

TO MAKE UP

Close the top and the bottom of the piece as follows: working with two strands of yarn and a blunt-tipped sewing up needle, insert the needle through the edge st of every 4th row-end, pulling up tightly each time to gather, until there is only a small hole in the middle. Start to join the cast on edge to cast off edge, but only for about 5cm (2in) at each end, if you join any further you will not be able to insert the duvet. Roll the duvet into a pouffe shape and insert it into the knitted piece trying to make as even a shape as possible. Continue to join the seam until it is complete. You do not need to use a duvet, you could also use old pillows, cushions or even old knitwear, just make sure whatever you use is clean.

Heated Neck Pillow

This neck pillow will help you to achieve a moment of restorative relaxation every night of the week. Reap comfort from the combination of a weighty pillow, paired with the indulgently soft cashmere blend and mingled with the heady smell of the lavender. Shrug off all the aches and pains that you have accumulated over the long day by draping the pillow over the back of your neck and switching off from the stresses of daily life. Trust me, you will be unable to resist this pillow's soothing powers.

SIZE

Approximately 12 x 44cm (4³/₄ x 17¹/₄in)

MATERIALS

* 2 x 50g balls of Debbie Bliss Cashmerino Aran in grey
* Pair of 4.50mm (US 7) knitting needles
* 27 x 47cm (10³/₄ x 18¹/₂in) piece of muslin or other fine cotton fabric
* Sewing thread
* Cleaned and dried cherry stones (www.cottonbarons.co.uk)
* Optional dried lavender or lavender essential oil

TENSION

22 sts and 32 rows to 10cm (4in) square over patt using 4.50mm (US 7) needles.

ABBREVIATIONS

wyif with yarn in front.
Also see page 11.

COVER

With 4.50mm (US 7) needles, cast on 97 sts.

1st row (wrong side) [K1, p1] 3 times, * [k2, p1] twice, [k1, p1] twice; rep from * to last st, k1.

2nd row [K1, p1] twice, * k2, p1, wyif, sl 3 sts purlwise, p1, k2, p1; rep from * to last 3 sts, k1, p1, k1.

3rd row [K1, p1] 3 times, * k1, p3, [k1, p1] 3 times; rep from * to last st, k1.

4th row [K1, p1] twice, * k2, p1, k1, lift yarn strand with needle tip, k1, then take yarn strand over the stitch, k1, p1, k2, p1; rep from * to last 3 sts, k1, p1, k1.

These 4 rows **form** the pattern and are repeated throughout.

Work in patt until piece measures approximately 26cm (10¼in), ending with a 4th row.

Cast off in patt.

Join the cast on edge to the cast off edge.

With the seam lying centrally, join the row ends of one side.

PAD

Fold the fabric in half lengthwise and join the long side and across one short side. Fold the open end over onto wrong side and press. Turn through to the right side. Mix the lavender into the cherry stones and fill the pad, but not too full, just over halfway, so allowing for the pad to be gently shaped around the neck. Tuck the raw ends of the fabric inside and stitch across the width so enclosing the contents.

TO FINISH

Insert the filled pad into the knitted cover.

TO HEAT

Remove the pad from the knitted cover and heat either in a conventional oven on the lowest possible setting or for a minute or so in a microwave oven on a medium setting. Keep an eye on it and do not overheat.

Cocoon

Armchair Throw

This cosy throw has a wonderfully comforting texture and will brighten any armchair. I have made this in a luxurious purple with a contrasting red trim, but it will work in any combination of colours, so you can pick those that will suit your room. Perfect for curling up with, this throw will require a little time and a fair amount of wool, but it is an extremely simple pattern and the end result will prove it to be well worth the effort.

SIZE

Approximately 70 x 138cm (27½ x 54¼in)

MATERIALS

✳ 10 x 50g hanks of Debbie Bliss Paloma in cyclaman (M) and 3 x 50g hanks in ruby (C)
✳ One long 10mm (US 15) circular knitting needle

TENSION

11 sts and 19 rows to 10cm (4in) square over moss st using 10mm (US 15) needles.

ABBREVIATIONS

See page 11.

NOTE

When changing colour, twist yarns on wrong side to avoid holes.

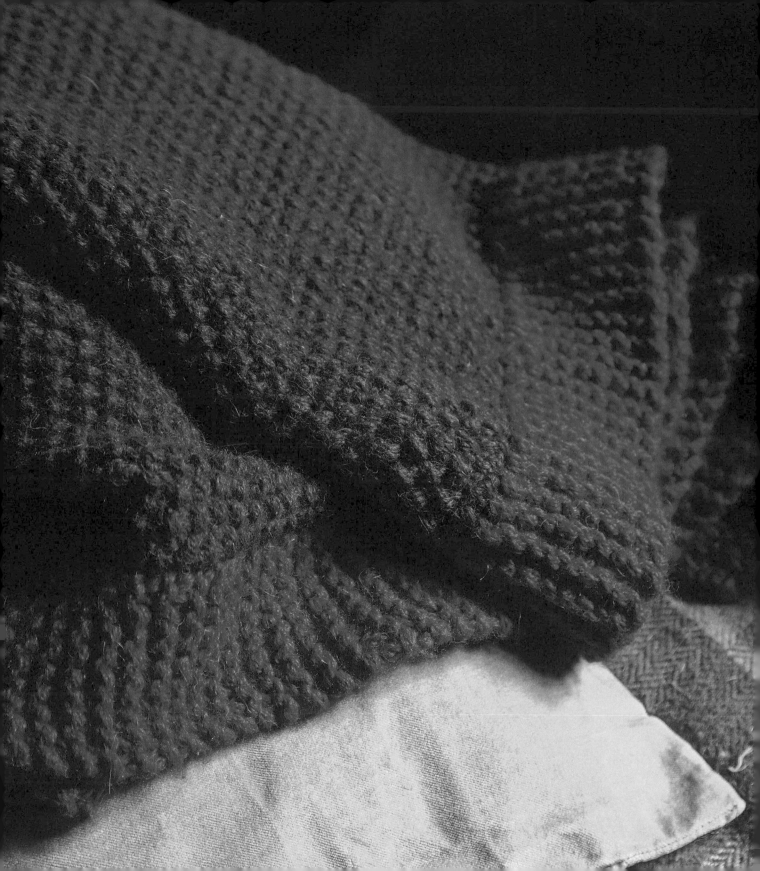

TO MAKE

With 10mm (US 15) circular needle and C, cast on 77 sts.

Work backwards and forwards in rows.

K 11 rows.

Now work in patt as follows:

1st row (right side) K9C, with M, k1, [p1, k1] to last 9 sts, k9C.

This row **forms** the moss st in main colour with garter st border in contrast colour and is repeated.

Cont in patt until work measures 132cm (52in) from cast on edge, ending with a wrong side row.

With C, k 10 rows.

Cast off.

Trapper Hat

Whilst out and about keep yourself nice and warm by wearing this fashionable trapper hat. Practical yet stylish, the hat has shaped earflaps and is lined with a layer of fur fabric to ensure the cold weather is kept at bay. Although this may appear a slightly complicated design, the making is actually split into different stages to prevent it being a daunting process. The earflaps and peak of the hat are knitted first then worked together with the crown.

SIZE
To fit medium sized adult head

MATERIALS
* 2 x 50g balls of Debbie Bliss Cashmerino Aran in ruby
* Pair of 5mm (US 8) knitting needles
* Approximately 51 x 84cm (18 x 33in) piece of black fur fabric for lining

TENSION
18 sts and 24 rows to 10cm (4in) square over st st using 5mm (US 8) needles.

ABBREVIATIONS
See page 11.

EARLFLAPS (make 2)

With 5mm (US 8) needles, cast on 10 sts.
Beg with a k row, work in st st and inc one st at each end of
2nd row and foll 5 rows. **22 sts.**
Work a further 19 rows without shaping.
Leave sts on a holder.

PEAK

With 5mm (US 8) needles, cast on 26 sts.
Beg with a k row, work in st st and inc one st at each end of
2nd row and foll 6 rows. **40 sts.**
Work a further 11 rows without shaping.
Leave sts on a holder.

CROWN

With 5mm (US 8) needles, cast on 8 sts, then k across 22 sts of
left earflap, cast on 5 sts, k across 40 sts of peak, cast on 5 sts,
k across 22 sts of right earflap, cast on 8 sts. **110 sts.**
Beg with a p row, work 4 rows in st st.
Next row (wrong side) K to end.
Now work in patt as follows:
1st row K3, [p1, k5] to last 5 sts, p1, k4.
2nd row P3, [k1, p1, k1, p3] to last 5 sts, k1, p1, k1, p2.
3rd row K1, [p1, k3, p1, k1] to last st, p1.
4th row K2, [p5, k1] to end.
5th row As 3rd row.
6th row As 2nd row.
These 6 rows **form** the patt and are repeated.
Patt a further 18 rows.
25th row (right side) K3, [p1, k1, k2tog, k2] to last 5 sts, p1, k1,
k2tog, k1. **92 sts**
Next row K to end.
Dec row K1, [k4, k2tog] to last st, k1. **77 sts.**
Next row P to end.
Dec row K1, [k3, k2tog] to last st, k1. **62 sts.**
Next row P to end.

Dec row K1, [k2, k2tog] to last st, k1. **47 sts.**
Next row P to end.
Dec row K1, [k1, k2tog] to last st, k1. **32 sts.**
Next row P to end.
Dec row K1, [k2tog] to last st, k1. **17 sts.**
Dec row P2, [p2tog] to last st, p1. **10 sts.**
Break yarn, thread end through rem sts, pull up and secure.

TO LINE AND MAKE UP

Lay the knitted piece onto the fur fabric lining and cut around
the edge, adding 5mm (³/₈in) all around. Make darts to shape
the top of the fabric to mimic the crown of the hat and trim
away the excess. Taking a whole stitch at each side into the
seam, join the back seam of the knitted piece. Make 2 twisted
cords 27cm (10¹/₂in) long, attach one to the edge of each
earflap. With right sides together, join the back seam of the
lining taking a 5mm (³/₈in) seam allowance, then turn lining to
right side, insert into the hat and folding approximately 5mm
(³/₈in) of lining onto the wrong side, slipstitch all around the
edges of the hat, earflaps and peak.

Slippers

Exceptionally plush and comfortable, these sweet little slippers are so impressive that a shop-bought pair is simply no comparison. Decorated with a beautiful zig-zag design executed in warm shades of ruby, burnt orange, blackberry, mulberry and gold and finished with a fun detail, a tassel, these slippers will undoubtably evoke a feeling of envy in all your family and friends. These are delightfully snug footwear that will keep your toes toasty and are well worth putting aside a little time to make.

SIZE
To fit ladies shoe size UK 5 (US 7½)

MATERIALS
* 1 x 50g ball of Debbie Bliss Cashmerino Aran in each of ruby (A), blackberry (B), gold (C), burnt orange (D) and mulberry (E)
* Pair of 5mm (US 8) knitting needles
* One 30cm (12in) square of felt
* Pair of ladies size UK 5 (US 7½) sheepskin insoles

TENSION
18 sts and 24 rows to 10cm (4in) square over st st using 5mm (US 8) needles.

ABBREVIATIONS
See page 11.

TO MAKE

With 5mm (US 8) needles and A, cast on 103 sts.

K 1 row.

Beg with a k row, work in st st as follows:

1st row (right side) With A, k to end.

2nd row With A, p to end.

3rd row [K5A, 1B] 8 times, k1A, k2tog A, k1A, skpo A, k1A, [k1B, k5A] 8 times. **101 sts.**

4th row P2A, [p1B, p1A, p3B, p1A] 7 times, p1B, p1A, p2B, p2tog tbl B, p1A, p2tog B, p2B, p1A, p1B, [p1A, p3B, p1A, p1B] 7 times, p2A. **99 sts.**

5th row K4B, [k1C, k1B, k1C, k3B] 7 times, k1C, k2tog B, k1C, skpo B, k1C, [k3B, k1C, k1B, k1C] 7 times, k4B. **97 sts.**

6th row P2C, [p1B, p5C] 7 times, p1B, p1C, p2tog tbl C, p1C, p2tog C, p1C, p1B, [p5C, p1B] 7 times, p2C. **95 sts.**

7th row [K2D, k1C] 15 times, k2tog D, k1D, skpo D, [k1C, k2D] 15 times. **93 sts.**

8th row [P5D, p1A] 7 times, p2D, p2tog tbl D, p1D, p2tog D, p2D, [p1A, p5D] 7 times. **91 sts.**

9th row K2D, [k1A, k1D, k3A, k1D] 6 times, k1A, k1D, k3A, k2tog D, k1A, skpo D, k3A, k1D, k1A, [k1D, k3A, k1D, k1A] 6 times, k2D. **89 sts.**

10th row P4A, [p1B, p1A, p1B, p3A] 6 times, p1B, p1A, p2tog tbl B, p1A, p2tog B, p1A, p1B, [p3A, p1B, p1A, p1B] 6 times, p4A. **87 sts.**

11th row K3A, [k2B, k1A] 12 times, k2B, k2tog B, k1B, skpo B, k2B, [k1A, k2B] 12 times, k3A. **85 sts.**

12th row [P2C, p1B] 13 times, p1C, p2tog tbl C, p1B, p2tog C, p1C, [p1B, p2C] 13 times. **83 sts.**

13th row K4C, [k3E, k3C] 5 times, k3E, k2C, k2tog C, k1C, skpo C, k2C, k3E, [k3C, k3E] 5 times, k4C. **81 sts.**

14th row P2E, [p1C, p5E] 6 times, p2tog tbl C, p1C, p2tog C, [p5E, p1C] 6 times, p2E. **79 sts.**

15th row K2D, [k1E, k2D] 11 times, k1E, k1D, k2tog D, k1E, skpo D, k1D, k1E, [k2D, k1E] 11 times, k2D. **77 sts.**

16th row P4A, [p3D, p3A] 5 times, p2D, p2tog tbl D, p1A, p2tog D, p2D, [p3A, p3D] 5 times, p4A. **75 sts.**

17th row K5A, [k1D, k5A] 5 times, k2tog D, k1A, skpo D, [k5A, k1D] 5 times, k5A. **73 sts.**

18th row P34A, p2tog tbl A, p1A, p2tog A, p34A. **71 sts.**

19th row (right side) P33A, p2tog A, p1A, p2tog tbl A, p33A. **69 sts.**

Cast off knitwise.

TO FINISH

Join back seam.

Using the sheepskin insoles as a guide, draw around the edge, adding a 5mm (³⁄₈in) seam allowance, to make a paper template. Then cut two pieces of felt using the template. Mark the centre of the heel edge. Stitch the cast on edge of the slipper to the felt, making sure the back seam matches the heel marker. Insert the insole into the slipper. Make a small tassel from yarn and sew to the top of the back seam.

Slouchy Hat

Perfectly suited to the cooler seasons, this fashionable hat is extremely simple to make and economical as it requires only a few balls of yarns to make. Worked in extra fine merino wool in an aran-weight yarn, this hat has a wonderfully silky texture and is gorgeously soft to the touch – qualities ideal for this project as the extra fine wool creates the desired slouch at the back of the hat as well as having enough stretch to ensure it will comfortably fit.

SIZE
One size to fit an average sized adult head

MATERIALS
✱ 3 x 50g balls of Debbie Bliss Rialto Aran in royal (A) and 1 x 50g ball in red (B)
✱ Pair each 4mm (US 6) and 5mm (US 8) knitting needles

TENSION
18 sts and 24 rows to 10cm (4in) square over st st using 5mm (US 8) needles.

ABBREVIATIONS
See page 11.

TO MAKE

With 4mm (US 6) needles and B, cast on 102 sts.

1st rib row (right side) P1, [k1, p1, k1, p2] to last st, k1.

2nd rib row P1, [k2, p1, k1, p1] to last st, k1.

These 2 rows **form** the rib and are repeated.

Rib a further 9 rows, so ending with 1st rib row.

Inc row (wrong side) P1, [k2, p1, k1, m1, p1] to last st, k1. **122 sts.**

Change to 5mm (US 8) needles.

Change to A.

1st row K to end.

2nd row P1, [k2, p1] to last st, k1.

3rd row P1, [k1, p2] to last st, k1.

These last 2 rows **form** the rib and are repeated.

Rib a further 43 rows, ending with a 2nd rib row.

Dec row P1, [k1, p2, k1, p2tog] to last st, k1. **102 sts.**

Work a further 3 rows in rib as set.

Dec row P1, [k1, p2tog, k1, p1] to last st, k1. **82 sts.**

Work a further 3 rows in rib as set.

Dec row P1, * sl 1, k2tog, psso, p1, [k1, p1] twice; rep from * to last st, k1. **62 sts.**

Work a further 3 rows in rib as set.

Dec row P1, [k1, p1, k1, p3tog] to last st, k1. **42 sts.**

Work a further 3 rows in rib as set.

Dec row P1, * sl 1, k2tog, psso, p1; rep from * to last st, k1. **22 sts.**

Next row P1, [p2tog] 10 times, p1. **12 sts.**

Break off yarn, thread through rem sts, pull up and secure, then join seam.

Chair Back

Give your chairs a new lease of life with these ingenius knitted covers. These covers do take a while to make so set aside plenty of me-time, especially if you are planning to make a set. The chunky cable knit fabric will last well with prolonged wear and give added comfort to your seating. The stylish leather ties that run down both sides add textural contrast, and ensures the knit holds a good shape over time.

SIZE
One size approximately 43 x 96cm (17 x 37¾ in)

MATERIALS
✳ 10 x 50g balls of Debbie Bliss Rialto Chunky in gold
✳ Pair of 6.50mm (US 10½) knitting needles
✳ Cable needle
✳ 2.2m (2½yd) of leather strip (or ribbon)

TENSION
15 sts and 21 rows to 10cm (4in) square over st st using 6.50mm (US 10½) needles.

ABBREVIATIONS
bind 3 yarn to back of work, sl 1, k1, yf, k1, pass the slipped st over the [k1, yf, k1].
MB pick up loop lying between st just worked and next st on left hand needle, k into back, front and back of loop, turn, p3, turn, k3, turn, p1, p2tog, turn, k2tog.

C4B slip next 2 sts onto cable needle and hold at back of work, k2, then k2 from cable needle.
C4F slip next 2 sts onto cable needle and hold to front of work, k2, then k2 from cable needle.
C6B slip next 3 sts onto cable needle and hold at back of work, k3, then k3 from cable needle.
C6F slip next 3 sts onto cable needle and hold to front of work, k3, then k3 from cable needle.
C3BP slip next st onto cable needle and hold at back of work, k2, then p1 from cable needle.
C3FP slip next 2 sts onto cable needle and hold to front of work, p1, then k2 from cable needle.
C4BP slip next st onto cable needle and hold at back of work, k3, then p1 from cable needle.
C4FP slip next 3 sts onto cable needle and hold to front of work, p1, then k3 from cable needle.
C5BP slip next 2 sts onto cable needle and hold at back of work, k3, then p2 from cable needle.
C5FP slip next 3 sts onto cable needle and hold to front of work, p2, then k3 from cable needle;
cluster 6 k next 6 sts and slip them onto a cable needle, wrap yarn 4 times anticlockwise round these 6 sts, slip sts back onto right hand needle.
Also see page 11.

PANEL A

This panel is worked over 20 sts.

1st row Bind 3, p4, k6, p4, bind 3.

2nd row P3, k4, p6, k4, p3.

3rd row Bind 3, p4, C6B, p4, bind 3.

4th row P3, k4, p6, k4, p3.

5th row Bind 3, p3, C4BP, C4FP, p3, bind 3.

6th row P3, k3, p3, k2, p3, k3, p3.

7th row C5FP, C4BP, p2, C4FP, C5BP.

8th row K2, p6, k4, p6, k2.

9th row P2, C6B, p4, C6F, p2.

10th row As 8th row.

11th row [C5BP, C5FP] twice.

12th row As 2nd row.

13th row K3, p1, cluster 6, p1, k3.

14th row As 2nd row.

15th row [C5FP, C5BP] twice.

16th to 18th rows As 8th to 10th rows.

19th row C5BP, C4FP, p2, C4BP, C5FP.

20th row As 6th row.

21st row Bind 3, p3, C4FP, C4BP, p3, bind 3.

22nd to 24th rows As 2nd to 4th rows.

25th to 28th rows Rep 1st and 2nd rows twice.

These 28 rows **form** the patt and are repeated throughout.

PANEL B

This panel is worked over 40 sts.

1st row P3, MB, p1, pass bobble st over the p1, p2, k4, [p4, MB, p1, pass bobble st over the p1, p3, k4] twice, p3, MB, p1, pass bobble st over the p1, p2.

2nd row K6, p4, [k8, p4] twice, k6.

3rd row P6, C4B, [p8, C4B] twice, p6.

4th row K6, p4, [k8, p4] twice, k6.

5th row P5, C3BP, C3FP, [p6, C3BP, C3FP] twice, p5.

6th row K5, p2, k2, p2, [k6, p2, k2, p2] twice, k5.

7th row P4, [C3BP, p2, C3FP, p4] 3 times.

8th row K4, [p2, k4] 6 times.

9th row P3, C3BP, p4, C3FP, [p2, C3BP, p4, C3FP] twice, p3.

10th row K3, p2, k6, p2, [k2, p2, k6, p2] twice, k3.

11th row P2, [C3BP, p6, C3FP] 3 times, p2.

12th row K2, [p2, k8, p2] 3 times, k2.

13th row P2, k2, p8, [C4B, p8] twice, k2, p2.

14th row As 12th row.

15th row P2, k2, p4, MB, p1, pass bobble st over the p1, p3, [k4, p4, MB, p1, pass bobble st over the p1, p3] twice, k2, p2.

16th to 18th rows As 12th to 14th rows.

19th row P2, [C3FP, p6, C3BP] 3 times, p2.

20th row As 10th row.

21st row P3, C3FP, p4, C3BP, [p2, C3FP, p4, C3BP] twice, p3.

22nd row As 8th row.

23rd row P4, [C3FP, p2, C3BP, p4] 3 times.

24th row As 6th row.

25th row P5, C3FP, C3BP, [p6, C3FP, C3BP] twice, p5.

26th row As 4th row.

27th row P6, C4B, [p8, C4B] twice, p6.

28th row K6, p4, [k8, p4] twice, k6.

These 28 rows **form** the patt and are repeated throughout.

TO MAKE

With 6.50mm (US 10½) needles, cast on 77 sts.

P 3 rows.

Inc row P5, k4, p1, m1, p2, m1, p1, k4, p3, k6, p2, m1, p1, [k8, p2, m1, p1] twice, k6, p3, k4, p1, m1, p2, m1, p1, k4, p5. **84 sts.**

Now work in patt as follows:

1st row (right side) P2, work across 1st row of Panels A, B, A, p2.

2nd row P2, work across 2nd row of Panels A, B, A, p2.

These 2 rows **set** the panels with garter st edges.

Cont in patt until work measures 95cm (37½in) from cast on edge, ending with a 1st patt row.

Dec row P5, k4, p1, [p2tog] twice, p1, k4, p3, k6, p1, p2tog, p1, [k8, p1, p2tog, p1] twice, k6, p3, k4, p1, [p2tog] twice, p1, k4, p5. **77 sts.**

P 2 rows.

Cast off purlwise.

TO FINISH

Cut the leather strip into 8 equal lengths and with the knitted piece placed over the chair, thread the leather strip through the edges of the knitting and tie to hold in place.

Snood

Over the past few years, the snood has cemented its place as a wardrobe staple and is an essential accessory for the ever too frequent cold weather. Staying away from the dreary blacks, browns and greys that often dominate autumn and winter wardrobes, instead I have used a refreshing and somewhat surprising combination of colours – a bright pink teamed with a burnt orange. Knitted in my favourite moss stitch, there is no shaping required for this simple snood.

SIZE
Approximately 35cm (13¾in) wide x 100cm (43¼in) long

MATERIALS
✱ 3 x 50g hanks of Debbie Bliss Paloma in each of hot pink (A) and burnt orange (B)
✱ Pair of 15mm (US 19) knitting needles

TENSION
7.5 sts and 12 rows to 10cm (4in) square over moss st using 15mm (US 19) needles and two strands of yarn used together.

ABBREVIATIONS
See page 11.

TO MAKE

With 15mm (US 19) needles and one strand of A and one strand of B used together, cast on 26 sts.

1st row (right side) [K1, p1] to end.

2nd row [P1, k1] to end.

These 2 rows **form** the moss st and are repeated.

Cont in patt until piece measures approximately 100cm (43¼in) or until you have just enough yarn remaining to work the cast off row.

Cast off in moss st.

TO FINISH

Join cast on and cast off edges together.

Cabled Socks

A treat for your feet, these cabled socks are a touch of pure luxury. Not only stylish, with attached pompons they are great fun too! Made from supple Baby Cashmerino and knitted in a simple yet effective cable knit, these socks are perfect for lazing around the house and look cheeky peeking out the top of a pair of boots. In fact these are so comfy it will be hard to make yourself take these off at the end of the day so you will probably end up wearing them to bed too!

SIZE
To fit ladies shoe size UK 4–5 (5–6)/ US 6½–7½ (7½–8½)

TENSION
25 sts and 34 rows to 10cm (4in) square over st st using 3.25mm (US 3) needles.

MATERIALS
* 6(7) x 50g balls of Debbie Bliss Baby Cashmerino in sienna
* Pair of 3.25mm (US 3) knitting needles
* Set of four 3.25mm (US 3) double pointed knitting needles
* Cable needle

ABBREVIATIONS
C11B slip next 6 sts onto cable needle and hold at back of work, k5, slip the purl st back onto left hand needle, p this st, then k5 from cable needle.
C2BP slip next st onto cable needle and hold at back of work, k1, then p1 from cable needle.
C2FP slip next st onto cable needle and hold to front of work, p1, then k1 from cable needle.
Also see page 11.

TO MAKE

With 3.25mm (US 3) needles, cast on 79 sts.

1st row (right side) K2, [p2, C2BP, k1, C2FP, p2, k2] to end.

2nd row P2, [k2, p1, k1, p1, k1, p1, k2, p2] to end.

3rd row K2, [p1, C2BP, p1, k1, p1, C2FP, p1, k2] to end.

4th row P2, [k1, p1, k2, p1, k2, p1, k1, p2] to end.

5th row K2, [C2BP, p2, k1, p2, C2FP, k2] to end.

6th row P2, [p1, k3, p1, k3, p3] to end.

Rep the last 6 rows 3 times more and the first 5 rows again.

Inc row (wrong side) P1, m1, p1, [p1, k1, m1, k1, m1, k1, p1, k1, m1, k1, m1, k1, p2, m1, p1] to end. **115 sts.**

Now work in cable patt as follows:

1st row K3, [p1, k5, p1, k5, p1, k3] to end.

2nd row P3, [k1, p5, k1, p5, k1, p3] to end.

3rd to 6th rows Rep 1st and 2nd rows twice more.

7th row K3, [p1, C11B, p1, k3] to end.

8th row As 2nd row.

9th to 14th rows Rep 1st and 2nd rows 3 times.

These 14 rows **form** the patt and are repeated.

Work straight until sock measures 35cm (14in), ending with a 6th row.

Dec row K1, k2tog, * p1, slip next 6 sts onto cable needle and hold at back of work, [k next st from left hand needle tog with 1 st on cable needle] 5 times, slip 'p' st back onto left hand needle, p this st tog with next st on left hand needle, k2tog, k1; rep from * to end. **65 sts.**

Next row P2, [k1, p5, k1, p2] to end.

Next row K2, [p1, k5, p1, k2] to end.

Rep the last 2 rows once more.

Next row P2, [k1, p1, p2tog, p2, k1, p2] to end. **58 sts.**

Next row K2, [p1, k4, p1, k2] to end.

Next row P2tog, [k1, p4, k1, p2] to last 7 sts, k1, p3, k1, p2tog. **56 sts.**

Break yarn.

Divide sts onto 3 double pointed needles as follows: slip first 14 sts onto first needle, next 14 sts onto second needle and next 14 sts onto 3rd needle, slip last 14 sts onto other end of first needle.

Heel flap

With right side facing, join yarn to 28 sts on first needle. Work on these 28 sts only.

Beg with a k row, work 15 rows in st st.

Shape heel

**** Next row** Sl 1, p to end.

Next row Sl 1, k16, skpo, k1, turn.

Next row Sl 1, p7, p2tog, p1, turn.

Next row Sl 1, k8, skpo, k1, turn.

Next row Sl 1, p9, p2tog, p1, turn.

Next row Sl 1, k10, skpo, k1, turn.

Next row Sl 1, p11, p2tog, p1, turn.

Next row Sl 1, k12, skpo, k1, turn.

Next row Sl 1, p13, p2tog, p1, turn.

Next row Sl 1, k14, skpo, k1, turn.

Next row Sl 1, p15, p2tog, p1, turn. **18 sts.**

Foot shaping

With right side facing, k18, pick up and k12 sts along side of heel flap, place a marker, k28 from 2nd and 3rd needles, place a marker, pick up and k12 sts along other side of heel flap. **70 sts.**

Arrange these sts evenly on 3 needles and cont in rounds as follows:

Round 1 K to within 2 sts of marker, k2tog, slip marker, k to next marker, slip marker, skpo, k to end.

Round 2 K to end.

Rep the last 2 rounds 6 times more. **56 sts.**

Slipping markers on every round, work straight until sock measures 18(19)cm/7(7½)in from back of heel.

Shape toe

Round 1 K to within 3 sts of marker k2tog, k1, slip marker, k1, skpo, k to within 3 sts of next marker, k2tog, k1, slip marker, k1, skpo, k to end.

Round 2 K to end.

Rep the last 2 rounds until 32 sts rem.

Slip first 8 sts onto one needle, next 16 sts onto a second needle, then rem 8 sts onto end of first needle.

Transfer the two groups of sts onto safety pins, fold sock inside out, then transfer the sts back onto two needles and cast off one st from each needle together. Sew cuff, leg and ankle seam. Make two twisted cords approximately 64cm (25in) long. Make four pompons. Weave each cord in and out around the sock just below the cuff and attach the pompons to each end.

Waterfall Jacket

The tumbling, rippling lapels of this soft unstructured jacket echo the undulations of water, hence its name. Made in a blended yarn of baby alpaca and silk, the jacket is so warming and enveloping that you simply will not ever want to take it off. Worked in stocking stitch, with moss stitch borders for just a hint of texture, this garment only needs minimal shaping so is a breeze to make. And the roomy patch pockets are the perfect hiding place for indulgent treats.

SIZE

To fit bust

81	86	92	97	102	107	112	117	cm
32	34	36	38	40	42	44	46	in

Finished measurements

Width across back

51	54	57.5	59.5	62	65	67.5	70	cm
20	21¼	22½	23	24½	25½	26¾	27½	in

Length to shoulder

75	76	77	78	79	80	81	82	cm
29½	30	30¼	30¼	31	31¼	32	32¼	in

Sleeve length 43cm (17in) for all sizes

MATERIALS

* 21(22:23:24:25:26:27:28) x 50g hanks of Debbie Bliss Andes in maroon
* Pair each 3.25mm (US 3) and 4mm (US 6) knitting needles
* One 3.25mm (US 3) circular knitting needle

TENSION

22 sts and 30 rows to 10cm (4in) square over st st using 4mm (US 6) needles.

ABBREVIATIONS

See page 11.

BACK

With 3.25mm (US 3) needles, cast on
115 (121:127:133:139:145:151:157) sts.
Moss st row (right side) K1, [p1, k1] to end.
Rep this row for 6cm (2¼in), ending with a wrong side row.
Change to 4mm (US 6) needles.
Beg with a k row, work in st st until back measures 56cm (22in) from cast on edge, ending with a p row.
Shape armholes
Cast off 6 (6:7:7:8:8:9:9) sts at beg of next 2 rows.
103 (109:113:119:123:129:133:139) sts.
Next row K2, skpo, k to last 4 sts, k2tog, k2.
Next row P to end.
Rep the last 2 rows 4 (5:5:6:6:7:7:8) times.
93 (97:101:105:109:113:117:121) sts.
Cont straight until back measures 73 (74:75:76:77:78:79:80)cm/
28¾(29¼:29½:30:30¼:30¾:31:31½)in from cast on edge, ending with a p row.
Shape upper arms and shoulders
Cast off 4 sts at beg of next 8 rows. 61 (65:69:73:77:81:85:89) sts.
Cast off 6 (6:7:7:8:8:9:9) sts at beg of next 2 rows and
6 (7:7:8:8:9:9:10) sts at beg of foll 2 rows.
Leave rem 37 (39:41:43:45:47:49:51) sts on a holder.

POCKET LININGS (make 2)

With 4mm (US 6) needles, cast on 31 (31:31:31:33:33:33:33) sts.
Beg with a k row, work 30 rows in st st.
Leave these sts on a spare needle.

LEFT FRONT

With 3.25mm (US 3) needles, cast on
121 (125:129:133:137:141:145:149) sts.
Moss st row (right side) K1, [p1, k1] to end.
Rep this row for 6cm (2¼in), ending with a wrong side row.
Change to 4mm (US 6) needles.
1st row K to last 9 sts, moss st 9.
2nd row Moss st 9, p to end.
These 2 rows **form** the st st with moss st border and are repeated.
Work a further 82 rows.

Place pocket

Next row K31 (33:35:37:38:40:42:44), slip next 31 (31:31:31:33:33:33:33) sts onto a holder, k across 31 (31:31:31:33:33:33:33) sts of first pocket lining, k50 (52:54:56:57:59:61:63), moss st 9.
Work straight until front measures 56cm (22in) from cast on edge, ending with a wrong side row.
Shape armhole
Next row Cast off 6 (6:7:7:8:8:9:9) sts, k to last 9 sts, moss st 9.
115 (119:122:126:129:133:136:140) sts.
Next row Moss st 9, p to end.
Next row K2, skpo, k to last 9 sts, moss st 9.
Rep the last 2 rows 4 (5:5:6:6:7:7:8) times.
110 (113:116:119:122:125:128:131) sts.
Cont straight until front measures same as Back to upper arm and shoulder shaping, ending at armhole edge.
Shape upper arm and shoulder
Cast off 4 sts at beg of next row and 3 foll right side rows.
94 (97:100:103:106:109:112:115) sts.
Work 1 row.
Cast off 6 (6:7:7:8:8:9:9) sts at beg of next row and
6 (7:7:8:8:9:9:10) sts at beg of foll right side row.
Work 1 row.
Leave rem 82 (84:86:88:90:92:94:96) sts on a holder.

RIGHT FRONT

With 3.25mm (US 3) needles, cast on
121 (125:129:133:137:141:145:149) sts.
Moss st row (right side) K1, [p1, k1] to end.
Rep this row for 6cm (2¼in), ending with a wrong side row.
Change to 4mm (US 6) needles.
1st row Moss st 9, k to end.
2nd row P to last 9 sts, moss st 9.
These 2 rows **form** the st st with moss st border and are repeated.

Work a further 82 rows.

Place pocket

Next row Moss st 9, k50(52:54:56:57:59:61:63), slip next 31(31:31:31:33:33:33:33) sts onto a holder, k across 31(31:31:31:33:33:33:33) sts of second pocket lining, k31(33:35:37:38:40:42:44).

Work straight until front measures 56cm (22in) from cast on edge, ending with a right side row.

Shape armhole

Next row Cast off 6(6:7:7:8:8:9:9) sts, patt to end. 115(119:122:126:129:133:136:140) sts.

Next row Moss st 9, k to last 4 sts, k2tog, k2.

Next row P to last 9 sts, moss st 9.

Rep the last 2 rows 4(5:5:6:6:7:7:8) times. 110(113:116:119:122:125:128:131) sts.

Cont straight until front measures same as Back to upper arm and shoulder shaping, ending at armhole edge.

Shape upper arm and shoulder

Cast off 4 sts at beg of next row and 3 foll wrong side rows. 94(97:100:103:106:109:112:115) sts.

Work 1 row.

Cast off 6(6:7:7:8:8:9:9) sts at beg of next row and 6(7:7:8:8:9:9:10) sts at beg of foll wrong side row.

Work 1 row.

Leave rem 82(84:86:88:90:92:94:96) sts on a holder.

SLEEVES

With 3.25mm (US 3) needles, cast on 41(43:45:47:49:51:53:55) sts.

Moss st row (right side) K1, [p1, k1] to end.

Rep this row for 6cm (2¼in), ending with a wrong side row.

Change to 4mm (US 6) needles.

Beg with a k row, work in st st.

Work 2 rows.

Inc row K3, m1, k to last 3 sts, m1, k3.

Work 5 rows.

Rep the last 6 rows 15 times more and the inc row again. 75(77:79:81:83:85:87:89) sts.

Cont straight until sleeve measures 43cm (17in) from cast on edge, ending with a p row.

Shape sleeve top

Cast off 6(6:7:7:8:8:9:9) sts at beg of next 2 rows. 63(65:65:67:67:69:69:71) sts.

Work 2 rows.

Next row K2, skpo, k to last 4 sts, k2tog, k2.

Work 3 rows.

Rep the last 4 rows once more.

Next row K2, skpo, k to last 4 sts, k2tog, k2.

Next row P to end.

Rep the last 2 rows 4(5:5:6:6:7:7:8) times. **49 sts.**

Cast off 3 sts at beg of next 12 rows.

Cast off rem 13 sts.

NECK EDGING

Join upper arm and shoulder seams.

With right side facing and 3.25mm (US 3) circular needle, slip 82(84:86:88:90:92:94:96) sts from right front holder onto a needle, k37(39:41:43:45:47:49:51) sts from back neck holder, then patt 82(84:86:88:90:92:94:96) sts from left front holder. **201(207:213:219:225:231:237:243) sts.**

Work 7 rows in moss st as set by front borders.

Cast off in moss st.

POCKET TOPS

With right side facing, slip 31(31:31:31:33:33:33:33) sts at top of pocket onto a 3.25mm (US 3) needle and work 7 rows in moss st.

Cast off in moss st.

TO MAKE UP

Join side and sleeve seams. Sew sleeves into armholes, easing to fit. Sew down pocket linings and pocket tops.

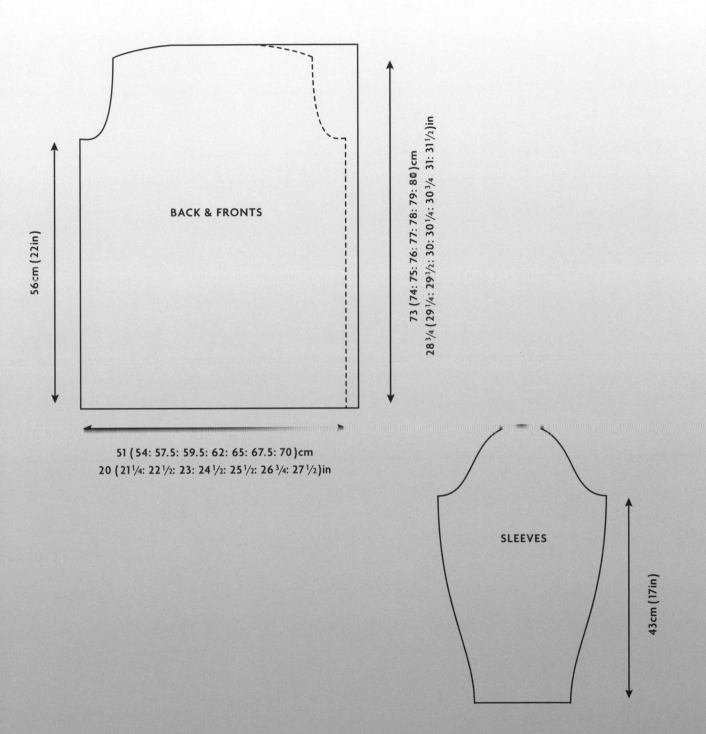

BACK & FRONTS

56cm (22in)

73 (74: 75: 76: 77: 78: 79: 80)cm
28³/₄ (29¹/₄: 29¹/₂: 30: 30¹/₄: 30³/₄: 31: 31¹/₂)in

51 (54: 57.5: 59.5: 62: 65: 67.5: 70)cm
20 (21¹/₄: 22¹/₂: 23: 24¹/₂: 25¹/₂: 26³/₄: 27¹/₂)in

SLEEVES

43cm (17in)

Detox

Accessories Holder

'A place for everything and everything in its place', this is an adage that, when lived by, can create a happy and harmonious home. This practical tie-up roll provides a stylish storage solution for knitters who need to keep tabs on their equipment. With pockets and divided sections for slotting pairs of knitting needles into as well as scissors, stitch counters and other accessories, including a sewn needlecase, this is a perfectly portable case that no knitter will want to be without.

SIZE
Approximately 30 x 39cm (12 x 15¼in)

MATERIALS
- ✱ 4 x 50g balls of Debbie Bliss Cotton DK in avocado
- ✱ Pair of 4.50mm (US 7) knitting needles
- ✱ 1m (1yd) of 15mm (⅝in) wide tape
- ✱ 0.5m (½yd) of fabric for lining (see Note)
- ✱ 18 x 22cm (7 x 8¾in) felt for needle case (optional)
- ✱ Sewing thread and needle

TENSION
24 sts and 26 rows to 10cm (4in) square over patt using 4.50mm (US 7) needles.

ABBREVIATIONS
See page 11.

NOTE
For the lining, we used Liberty Classic Tana Lawn in Claire-Aude T (www.liberty.co.uk).

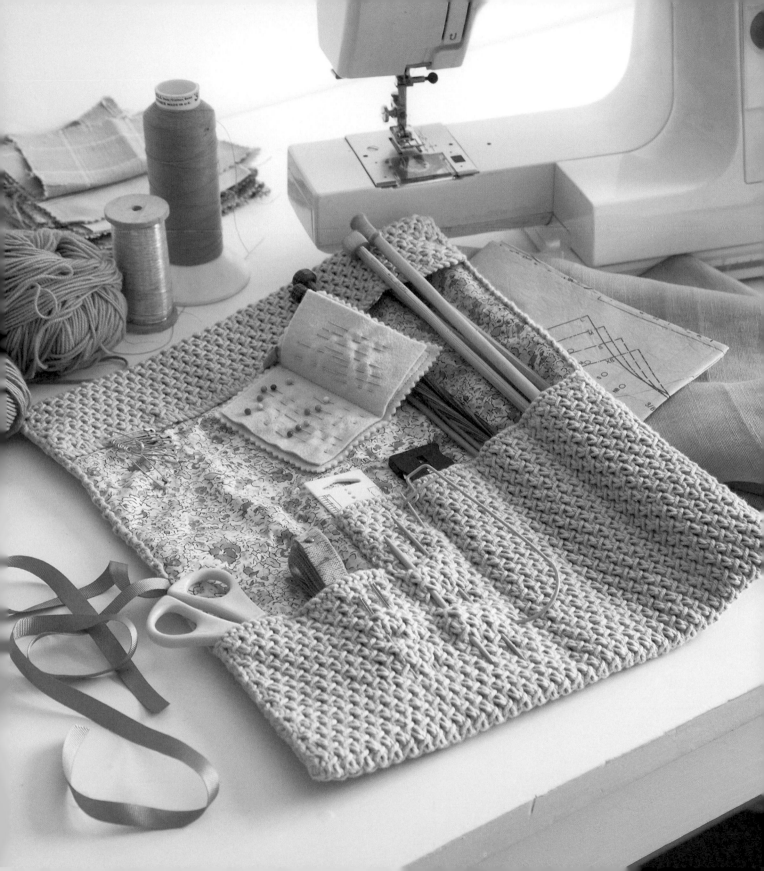

TO MAKE

With 4.50mm (US 7) needles, cast on 74 sts.

1st row (right side) K to end.

2nd row P1, [p2tog but do not slip st off needle, then p the first st again and slip both sts off needle together] to last st, p1.

3rd row K to end.

4th row P2, [p2tog but do not slip st off needle, then p the first st again and slip both sts off needle together] to last 2 sts, p2.

These 4 rows **form** the patt and are repeated throughout.

Work in patt until piece measures 56cm (22in), ending with a 3rd patt row.

Shape for pockets

Next row (wrong side) Cast off 26 sts knitwise, with 1 st on needle after cast off, p1, [p2tog but do not slip st off needle, then p the first st again and slip both sts off needle together] to last 2 sts, p2. **48 sts.**

Beg with a 1st row, cont in patt for a further 8cm (3¼in), ending with a right side row.

Cast off all sts knitwise.

TO MAKE UP

Using the knitted piece as a template, and making sure you place the wrong side of the lining fabric and wrong side of the knitting together, cut the lining fabric to shape, allowing a 1.5cm (⅝in) seam allowance all around. Cut a 5cm (2in) piece from the tape and reserve for the needle case (if making). Fold the remainder of the tape in two, approximately 30cm (12in) from one end. Press the seam allowance of the lining onto the wrong side, then folding the corners, handsew the fabric to the wrong side of the knitted piece, catching the fold of the tape into the seam, approximately 27cm (10¾in) down from cast on edge on the left hand side of the piece. Fold approximately 7cm (2¾in) of top (unshaped) edge over onto the fabric and slipstitch the sides in place from the fold down to the cast on edge. Fold the lower edge up onto the fabric, so that the final length of the completed holder will be 39cm (15¼in), and slipstitch the side edges in place. With sewing thread, stitch individual pockets in the lower section, these can be any width to suit your accessories.

NEEDLE CASE (optional)

Cut a piece of lining fabric and two pieces of felt, approximately 9 x 11cm (3½ x 4¼in). Fold under a 1cm (½in) seam allowance all around the fabric and press in place, mitring the corners. Fold the fabric in half and mark the centre line. Lay the hemmed fabric onto one piece of felt placing it centrally and topstitch around the edges, catching the short piece of tape into the seam to the left of the centre line. Lay the other piece of felt centrally on the first (inside of cover) and stitch through all layers along the centre line. Using pinking shears, trim the felt of the cover around the edge, then trim the inside piece of felt, slightly smaller, so that when closed, the inner felt does not show around the edge. Stitch the free end of the tape under the edge of the top flap of the holder.

Message Board

Whether used to hold messages for the rest of the household, notices of things to-do, useful clippings, photos of unforgettable moments or a combination of all these things, this clever message board will become an invaluable part of your life. Made using only one ball of yarn, this can easily be created in just a single afternoon. Pretty, simple and useful, this board can be adjusted for size and made in a variety of colours.

SIZE
60 x 40cm (24 x 16in)

MATERIALS
* ✷ 1 x 50g ball of Debbie Bliss Cotton DK in mink
* ✷ Pair of 3.75mm (US 5) knitting needles
* ✷ Approximately 70 x 50cm (28 x 20in) piece of fabric
* ✷ 60 x 40cm (24 x 16in) piece of felt or batting
* ✷ 600 x 400mm (24 x 16in) cork board (www.staples.co.uk)
* ✷ Staple gun and/or strong parcel tape
* ✷ Bronzed upholstery fix and fasten nails (www.ryman.co.uk)

ABBREVIATIONS
See page 11.

NOTES
The tension is not relevant.
Figures in brackets refer to the long lengths, figures before the brackets refer to the shorter lengths.
If you use a different size board, you will need to adjust the length of the strips, fabrics and the amount of yarn.
Our strips used one complete ball of yarn.

TO MAKE

Make 4 short lengths and 4 long lengths.

Leaving a 1.5(3)m/59(118)in length of yarn and using the thumb cast-on method throughout, work as follows:

Cast on row With 3.75mm (US 5) needles, place a slip knot on the right needle, [cast on 2 sts, lift the first st over the 2nd st and off needle, yrn, lift st over yrn, cast on one st] 38(76) times. 77(153) sts.

Cast off all sts knitwise.

TO FINISH

Cut the batting or felt to fit within the frame of the board and lay in place. Lay the fabric over the board, folding the excess over onto the back and neatly folding the corners. Then tape or staple the fabric in place to the back of the frame. Measure and mark (with pins) the positions for the knitted strips, then taking the excess over onto the back and pulling to tighten, staple the strips in place – four diagonally in one direction, then the remaining four diagonally in the other, weaving under and over. Apply the upholstery nails where the strips cross. If you prefer, you could also cover the back of the board with felt to neaten.

Double Moss Stitch Tunic

This pull-on tunic is worked in one of my favourite knitted stitches, double moss stitch. It produces a subtle texture that lends interest to this otherwise so simple top. Worked straight to form subtle capped sleeves and a slit neck, the ribbed hem brings the garment gently inwards at the lower edge. Around the neck and sleeve openings, I have added an integrated garter stitch edge.

MEASUREMENTS

To fit bust

81–86	92–97	102–107	112–117	cm
32–34	36–38	40–42	44–46	in

Finished measurements

Bust

98	106	118	126	cm
38½	41¾	46½	49½	in

Length to shoulder

76	78	80	82	cm
30	30¾	31½	32¼	in

MATERIALS

* 14(15:16:17) x 50g balls of Debbie Bliss Cotton DK in mint
* Pair of each 3.75mm (US 5) and 4mm (US 6) knitting needles
* 3.75mm (US 5) circular needle, 60cm (24in) long

TENSION

20 sts and 30 rows to 10cm (4in) square over double moss st using 4mm (US 6) needles.

ABBREVIATIONS

See page 11.

BACK

With 3.75mm (US 5) needles, cast on 98(106:118:126) sts.

1st row (right side) K2, [p2, k2] to end.

2nd row P2, [k2, p2] to end.

These 2 rows **form** the rib and are repeated.

Work a further 14 rows.

Change to 4mm (US 6) needles.

1st row (right side) K2, [p2, k2] to end.

2nd row P2, [k2, p2] to end.

3rd row P2, [k2, p2] to end.

4th row K2, [p2, k2] to end.

These 4 rows **form** the double moss st patt and are repeated.

Cont in patt until back measures 51(52:53:54)cm/ 20(20½:21:21¼)in from cast on edge, ending with a wrong side row. **

Now work in patt with garter st edgings as follows:

Next row K2, patt to last 2 sts, k2.

Rep the last row until back measures 76(78:80:82)cm/ 30(30¾:31½:32¼)in from cast on edge, ending with a wrong side row.

Shape shoulders

Cast off 6(6:7:7) sts at beg of next 8 rows and 10(13:13:16) sts at beg of foll 2 rows.

Leave rem 30(32:36:38) sts on a spare needle.

FRONT

Work as given for Back to **.

Divide for front opening

Now work in patt with garter st edgings as follows:

Next row (right side) K2, patt 46(50:56:60), k1, turn and work on these sts only for first side of front opening, leave rem sts on a spare needle.

Next row K1, patt to last 2 sts, k2.

Next row K2, patt to last st, k1.

The last 2 rows **form** the patt with garter st edging at front opening and armhole edge and are repeated.

Cont in patt until front measures 68(70:71:73)cm/ 26¾(27½:28:28¾)in from cast on edge, ending with a wrong side row.

Shape neck

Next row Patt to last 11 sts, place these 11 sts on a holder, turn and work on rem 38(42:48:52) sts for first side of front neck.

Patt 1 row.

Dec one st at neck edge on every right side row until 34(37:41:44) sts rem.

Work straight until front measures the same as Back to shoulder, ending at armhole edge.

Shape shoulder

Cast off 6(6:7:7) sts at beg of next row and 3 foll right side rows.

Work 1 row.

Cast off rem 10(13:13:16) sts.

With right side facing, rejoin yarn to rem sts.

Next row (right side) K1, patt to last 2 sts, k2.

Next row K2, patt to last st, k1.

These 2 rows **form** the patt with garter st edging at front opening and armhole edge.

Cont in patt until front measures 68(70:71:73)cm/ 26¾(27½:28:28¾)in from cast on edge, ending with a wrong side row.

Shape neck

Next row Patt 11 sts, leave these sts on a holder, patt to end. **38(42:48:52) sts.**

Patt 1 row.

Dec one st at neck edge on every right side row until 34(37:41:44) sts rem.

Work straight until front measures the same as Back to shoulder, ending at armhole edge.

Shape shoulder

Cast off 6(6:7:7) sts at beg of next row and 3 foll wrong side rows.

Work 1 row.

Cast off rem 10(13:13:16) sts.

NECK EDGING

Join shoulder seams.

With right side facing and 3.75mm (US 5) circular needle, place 11 sts from right front holder onto needle, pick up and k23(23:25:25) sts up right front neck, k30(32:36:38) sts from back neck holder, pick up and k23(23:25:25) sts down left front neck, patt 11 sts from right front holder. **98(100:108:110) sts.**

K 2 rows.

Cast off knitwise.

TO MAKE UP

Join side seams to beg of armhole edging.

BACK & FRONT

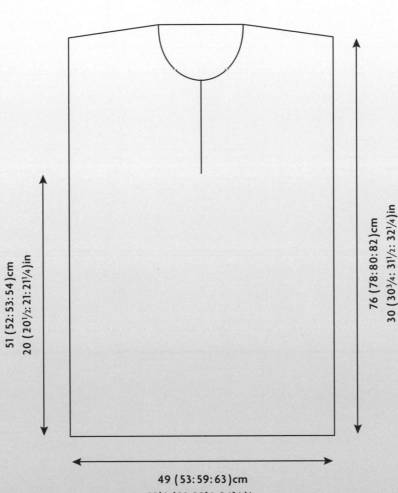

51 (52: 53: 54)cm
20 (20½: 21: 21¼)in

76 (78: 80: 82)cm
30 (30¾: 31½: 32¼)in

49 (53: 59: 63)cm
19¼ (21: 22¼: 24¾)in

Elizabeths Parrot

Hustle at 5pm

Storage File

Knitted in a robust cotton yarn, this filing system will transform
your storage options. I love the colourful organisation that this storage
file brings to my work shelves at home, but you do not need to only
keep your work and documents in it, you could also use it to store your
knitting patterns. Here, a lively aqua yarn that is accented with a pretty
lining is used, ensuring that sorting and storing
becomes anything but a chore.

SIZE
Approximately 22cm (8¾in) wide x
25cm (10in) high

TENSION
20½sts and 28 rows to 10cm (4in) over patt
using 4mm (US 6) needles.

MATERIALS
* 3 x 50g balls of Debbie Bliss Cotton DK
  in aqua
* Pair of 4mm (US 6) knitting needles
* Cardboard

ABBREVIATIONS
See page 11.

TO MAKE

With 4mm (US 6) needles, cast on 45 sts and k 1 row.

Now work in patt as follows:

1st row (right side) K1, [p1, k1] to end.

2nd row P1, [k1, p1] to end.

3rd row P1, [k1, p1] to end.

4th row K1, [p1, k1] to end.

These 4 rows **form** the irish moss st patt and are repeated.

Cont in patt until piece measures 10cm (4in) from cast on edge, ending with a right side row.

Foldline row K to end.

Beg with a 1st row, work 10cm (4in) in patt, ending with a right side row.

Foldline row (wrong side) Cast on 22 sts, k to end. **67 sts.**

Next row Cast on 22 sts, k1, [p1, k1] to end. **89 sts.**

Beg with a 2nd row, work in patt for 10cm (4in), ending with a 4th row.

Next row P2tog, patt to last 2 sts, p2tog.

Next row Patt to end.

Rep the last 2 rows until 45 sts rem, ending with a right side row.

Cast off knitwise.

DIVIDER

With 4mm (US 6) needles, cast on 43 sts.

Beg with a 1st row, work in patt until piece measures approximately 13cm (5in), ending with a right side row.

Cast off knitwise.

TO MAKE UP

Following the template, join edges B to B and D to D first, then join A to A and C to C.

TO FINISH

Using the template, cut the cardboard to shape; try to cut it out in one piece, but if that is not possible, cut the upper part (back and sides) in one piece, then cut out the lower part (base and front). Score the shape along the dotted lines and fold to form the file. Use parcel tape to fix the base and front to the back and sides. To form the divider, cut a piece of cardboard slightly smaller than the width of the inside of the file and to fit the length of the knitted divider piece. Using the template, cut the fabric to shape, adding 1.5cm (⅝in) around all the edges. Clip into the corner where side B meets base B and side D meets base D. Join edges B to B and D to D first, then join A to A and C to C. Press all seams, then insert lining into the constructed cardboard, folding the excess fabric over onto the outside of the box. Put the lined cardboard shape into the knitted piece and slipstitch the lining to the knitting around the edges. Cover the divider in the same way and slip into the box, catch stitch the top corners to the sides of the box.

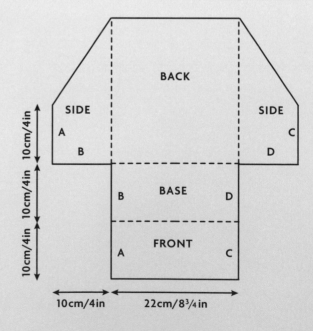

DETOX

Wine Bottle Covers

Rather than consign your glass bottles to the recycling, give them a new lease of life as covered vases with these witty knitted covers. Choose from the striped, cabled or fair isle styles – or mix and match to create a striking display. With a narrow neck, a bottle takes the agony out of flower arranging as no complicated structure or support is necessary. The beauty of these is that they take only a small amount of yarn in various colours, so can be made from the remnants of your yarn stash.

SIZE
One size to fit a standard 75cl wine bottle

MATERIALS
Striped Cover
* 1 x 50g ball Debbie Bliss Rialto 4ply in each of silver (A), teal (B), ecru (C), dark red (D), apple (E) and navy (F)

Fair Isle Cover
* 1 x 50g ball Debbie Bliss Rialto 4ply in each of silver (A), teal (B), ecru (C), dark red (D), apple (E) and navy (F)

Cable and Rib Cover
* 1 x 50g ball Debbie Bliss Rialto 4ply in ecru (C)
* Cable needle
* 3 small buttons

All covers
* Pair each of 3mm (US 2-3) and 3.25mm (US 3) knitting needles

TENSION
25 sts and 34 rows over st st, 29 sts and 34 rows over fair isle patt and 33 sts and 45 rows over cable patt, all to 10cm (4in) square using 3.25mm (US 3) needles.

YARN NOTE
If you are making all 3 covers, you will need a total of 2 x 50g balls in ecru (C) and 1 x 50g ball in each of the remaining 5 colours.

ABBREVIATIONS
See pages 11 and 104.

STRIPED COVER

With 3mm (US 2-3) needles and F, cast on 68 sts.

K 1 row.

Change to 3.25mm (US 3) needles.

Beg with a k row, work in st st and stripes of 2 rows A, 2 rows D, 2 rows B, 2 rows C, 2 rows E and 2 rows F.

Work straight until 76 rows have been worked.

Shape top

1st dec row (wrong side) P2, [p2tog, p6] 8 times, p2. **60 sts.**

K 1 row.

2nd dec row P2, [p2tog, p5] 8 times, p2. **52 sts.**

K 1 row.

3rd dec row P2, [p2tog, p4] 8 times, p2. **44 sts.**

K 1 row.

4th dec row P2, [p2tog, p3] 8 times, p2. **36 sts.**

K 1 row.

5th dec row P2, [p2tog, p2] 8 times, p2. **28 sts.**

Neck

Cont in stripe sequence and work a further 25 rows.

Cast off knitwise.

Join seam.

FAIRISLE COVER

With 3mm (US 2-3) needles and D, cast on 74 sts.

K 1 row.

Change to 3.25mm (US 3) needles.

Beg with a k row, work in st st and patt from chart until 61 rows have been worked.

Shape top

1st row With A, p2, [p2tog, p6] 9 times, p2. **65 sts.**

2nd row K2A, [1F, 6A] 9 times.

3rd row P5A, [3F, 4A] 8 times, 3 F, 1A.

4th row K2A, [1F, 6A] 9 times.

5th row With A, p2, [p2tog, p5] 9 times, p2.

6th row With A, k to end.

7th row P1A, [p2tog A, p1A, p1D, 1A, 1D] 9 times, 1A.

8th row With A, k to end.

9th row With A, p1, [p2tog, p3] 9 times, p1. **38 sts.**

10th row [K1B, k1A] to end.

11th row With A, p to end.

Collar

Cont in A only.

1st row K2, [p2, k2] to end.

2nd row P2, [k2, 2] to end.

Rep the last 2 rows for 21cm (8¼in).

Cast off in rib.

Join seam, reversing last 11cm (4¼in) of seam on collar.

Turn half of collar over.

CHART NOTE

Read chart from right to left on right side rows and left to right on wrong side rows. When working in pattern, strand yarn not in use loosely across wrong side of work to keep fabric elastic.

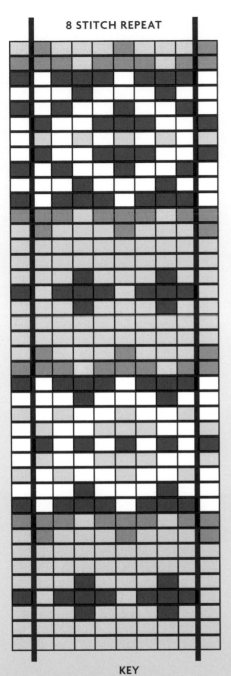

8 STITCH REPEAT

ABBREVIATIONS

C4B slip next 2 sts onto cable needle and hold at back of work, k2, then k2 from cable needle.

C4F slip next 2 sts onto cable needle and hold to front of work, k2, then k2 from cable needle.

Also see page 11.

CABLE COVER

With 3mm (US 2-3) needles and C, cast on 74 sts.

K 1 row.

Change to 3.25mm (US 3) needles and patt.

1st row K2, [p2, k6, p2, k2] to end.

2nd row P to end.

3rd row K2, [p2, C4B, k2, p2, k2] to end.

4th row P to end.

5th row K2, [p2, k2, C4F, p2, k2] to end.

6th row P to end.

The 3rd–6th rows **form** the patt and are repeated.

Work a further 84 rows, so ending with a 6th row.

Shape top

1st row K2, [p2tog, C4B, k2, p2tog, k2] to end. **62 sts.**

2nd row P to end.

3rd row K2, [p1, k2, slip next 2 sts onto a cable needle and hold to front of work, k2, then skpo from cable needle, p1, k2] to end. **56 sts.**

4th row P to end.

5th row K2, [p1, slip next 2 sts onto a cable needle and hold at back, k2tog, then k2 from cable needle, k1, p1, k2] to end. **50 sts.**

6th row P to end.

7th row K2, [p1, k1, slip next 2 sts onto a cable needle and hold at front, k1, then skpo from cable needle, p1, k2] to end. **44 sts.**

8th row P to end.

9th row K2, [p2tog, k1, p2tog, k2] to end. **32 sts.**

10th row P to end.

11th row K2, [p2tog, p1, k2] to end. **26 sts.**

12th row Cast on 3 sts for button band, p to end. **29 sts.**

Neck

1st row P4, [k2, p2] 5 times, k2, p3.

2nd row P to end.

3rd (buttonhole) row P1, p2tog, yrn, p1, [k2, p2] to last 5 sts, k2, p3.

4th row P to end.

5th to 18th rows Rep 1st and 2nd rows 7 times.

19th (buttonhole) row P1, p2tog, yrn, p1, [k2, p2] to last 5 sts, k2, p3.

20th row P to end.

21st to 34th rows Rep 1st and 2nd rows 7 times.

35th (buttonhole) row P1, p2tog, yrn, p1, [k2, p2] to last 5 sts, k2, p3.

36th row P to end.

37th row P4, [k2, p2] 5 times, k2, p3.

38th row P to end.

Cast off in patt.

Join side seam to beg of neck, sew cast on edge of button band behind bottom of buttonhole band. Sew on buttons.

Magazine Holder

Tired of forever having to clear up your widely scattered magazines and bored of tediously hunting for that magazine you kept because it contained that really great pattern? Then this sturdy magazine holder provides the perfect solution. Stylish, yet practical, this contemporary holder can store any manner of publications – whether for all your knitting, food or fashion magazines or even your newspapers. You may even find yourself making one in a different colour for each subject!

SIZE
Approximately 66 x 32cm (26 x 12 1/2 in)

MATERIALS
* 4 x 50g balls of Debbie Bliss Cotton DK in sea green
* Pair of 4mm (US 6) knitting needles
* 66 x 32cm (26 x 12 1/2 in) piece of pelmet weight buckram
* 69 x 35cm (27 1/4 x 13 3/4 in) piece of fabric
* Sewing thread
* Four 28cm (11in) lengths of 1cm (1/2 in) wide ribbon

TENSION
20 sts and 35 rows to 10cm (4in) square over main patt garter st using 4mm (US 6) needles.

ABBREVIATIONS
See page 11.

NOTE
Join on a new ball of yarn between the border and centre panel, not at the edge. The knitted piece will be slightly shorter than the buckram, to ensure a fit tight.

TO MAKE

With 4mm (US 6) needles, cast on 64 sts.

1st row (wrong side) K to end.

2nd row K to end.

3rd and 4th rows P to end.

These 4 rows **form** the border patt and are repeated 3 times more, so ending with a 4th row.

Now work in border and centre panel patt as follows:

1st row (wrong side) K11, p42, k11.

2nd row K11, p42, k11.

3rd and 4th rows P to end.

These 4 rows **form** the main patt with border at each side, and are repeated.

Work in patt until work measures 60cm (23¼in), ending with a 4th row.

Beg with a 1st row, work 16 rows in border patt across all sts.

Cast off purlwise.

TO MAKE UP

Cover one side of the buckram with fabric, folding in the excess. Arrange two lengths of ribbon evenly spaced along the short ends of the buckram and topstitch the fabric all around the edges, catching the ribbons into the seam. Lay the wrong side of the knitted piece onto the uncovered side of the buckram and slipstitch in place all around the edge. Tie the ribbons together to create a tube, then lay your magazines inside.

Extra Wide Cardigan

This fashionable slouch cardigan is perfect for every occasion and can be worn at home as well as out and about. It is made in one of my most luxurious yarns, Baby Cashmerino. This is a lightweight yarn with a cashmere blend, giving it a delightfully soft and comforting texture. It will take a little bit of time to achieve this cardigan and it is worth setting aside some quiet me-time to make, but your impressed family and friends will soon make it worth the effort.

MEASUREMENTS

To fit bust

81–86	92–97	102–107	112–117	cm
32–34	36–38	40–42	44–46	in

Finished measurements

Bust

130	141	153	164	cm
51¼	55½	60¼	64½	in

Length to shoulder

73	74.5	76.5	78	cm
28¾	29¼	30¼	30¾	in

Sleeve length

36cm (14¼in) for all sizes

MATERIALS

* 14 (15:16:17) x 50g balls of Debbie Bliss Baby Cashmerino in citrus
* Pair each 3mm (US 2-3) and 3.25mm (US 3) knitting needles
* One 3mm (US 2-3) circular knitting needle
* 9 buttons

TENSION

25 sts and 34 rows to 10cm (4in) square over st st using 3.25mm (US 3) needles.

ABBREVIATIONS

See page 11.

BACK

With 3mm (US 2-3) needles, cast on 165(179:193:207) sts.

1st rib row K1, [p1, k1] to end.

2nd rib row P1, [k1, p1] to end.

Rep the last 2 rows 4 times more.

Change to 3.25mm (US 3) needles.

Beg with a k row, work in st st until back measures 40cm (15¾in) from cast on edge, ending with a p row.

Shape underarms and raglans

Cast off 5(7:9:11) sts at beg of next 2 rows. **155(165:175:185) sts.**

Next row K2, skpo, k to last 4 sts, k2tog, k2.

Next row P to end.

Rep the last 2 rows 54(57:60:63) times more. **45(49:53:57) sts.**

Change to 3mm (US 2-3) needles.

1st rib row P1, [k1, p1] to end.

2nd rib row K1, [p1, k1] to end.

Rep the last 2 rows 3 times more.

Cast off in rib.

LEFT FRONT

With 3mm (US 2-3) needles, cast on 79(85:91:97) sts.

1st rib row P1, [k1, p1] to end.

2nd rib row K1, [p1, k1] to end.

Rep the last 2 rows 4 times more.

Change to 3.25mm (US 3) needles.

Beg with a k row, work in st st until front measures 40cm (15¾in) from cast on edge, ending with a p row.

Shape underarm, front neck and raglan

1st row Cast off 5(7:9:11) sts, k to last 4 sts, k2tog, k2. **73(77:81:85) sts.**

Next row P to end.

Next row K2, skpo, k to end.

Next row P2, p2tog, p to end.

Next row K2, skpo, k to end.

Next row P to end.

Next row K2, skpo, k to last 4 sts, k2tog, k2.

Next row P to end.

Rep the last 6 rows 6(6:7:7) times more. **38(42:41:45) sts.**

2nd and 4th sizes only

Next row K2, skpo, k to end.

Next row P2, p2tog, p to end. –(40:–:43) sts.

All sizes

Next row K2, skpo, k to end.

Next row P to end.

Rep the last 2 rows until 4 sts rem ending with a p row.

Leave these sts on a safety pin.

RIGHT FRONT

With 3mm (US 2-3) needles, cast on 79(85:91:97) sts.

1st rib row P1, [k1, p1] to end.

2nd rib row K1, [p1, k1] to end.

Rep the last 2 rows 4 times more.

Change to 3.25mm (US 3) needles.

Beg with a k row, work in st st until front measures 40cm (15¾in) from cast on edge, ending with a p row.

Shape underarm, front neck and raglan

Next row K2, skpo, k to end.

Next row Cast off 5(7:9:11) sts, p to end. **73(77:81:85) sts.**

Next row K to last 4 sts, k2tog, k2.

Next row P to last 4 sts, p2tog tbl, p2.

Next row K to last 4 sts, k2tog, k2.

Next row P to end.

Next row K2, skpo, k to last 4 sts, k2tog, k2.

Next row P to end.

Rep the last 6 rows 6(6:7:7) times more. **38(42:41:45) sts.**

2nd and 4th sizes only

Next row K to last 4 sts, k2tog, k2.

Next row P to last 4 sts, p2tog tbl, p2. –(40:–:43) sts.

All sizes

Next row K to last 4 sts, k2tog, k2.

Next row P to end.

Rep the last 2 rows until 4 sts rem.

Leave these sts on a safety pin.

SLEEVES

With 3mm (US 2-3) needles, cast on 53(59:65:71) sts.

1st rib row P1, [k1, p1] to end.

2nd rib row K1, [p1, k1] to end.

Rep the last 2 rows 4 times more.

Change to 3.25mm (US 3) needles.

Beg with a k row, work in st st.

Work 8 rows.

Inc row K3, m1, k to last 3 sts, m1, k3.

Work 5 rows.

Rep the last 6 rows 13(14:15:16) times more and the inc row again. 83(91:99:107) sts.

Work straight until sleeve measures 36cm (14¼in) from cast on edge, ending with a p row.

Shape raglans

Cast off 5(7:9:11) sts at beg of next 2 rows. 73(77:81:85) sts.

Next row K to end.

Next row P to end.

Next row K2, skpo, k to last 4 sts, k2tog, k2.

Next row P to end.

Rep the last 4 rows 23(25:27:29) times more. 25(25:25:25) sts.

Next row (right side) K2, skpo, k to last 4 sts, k2tog, k2.

Next row P to end.

Rep the last 2 rows until 11(13:15:17) sts rem, ending with a p row.

Leave these sts on a holder.

POCKETS (make 2)

With 3.25mm (US 3) needles, cast on 45(49:53:57) sts.

Beg with a k row, work 50(52:54:56) rows in st st.

Change to 3mm (US 2-3) needles.

1st rib row P1, [k1, p1] to end.

2nd rib row K1, [p1, k1] to end.

Rep the last 2 rows twice more.

Cast off in rib.

RIGHT FRONT AND NECK EDGING

With right side facing and 3mm (US 2-3) circular needle, pick up and k100 sts up right front edge from cast on edge to start of neck shaping, 89(93:97:101) sts up neck shaping to top of raglan, k3 sts from safety pin, k last st tog with first st of right sleeve, then k rem 10(12:14:16) sts across right sleeve. 203(209:215:221) sts.

1st row P1, [k1, p1] to end.

2nd row P2, k1, [p1, k1] to end.

These 2 rows **form** the rib and are repeated.

Work 1 more row.

Buttonhole row (right side) Rib 3, yf, work 2tog, [rib 9, yf, work 2tog] 8 times, rib to end.

Rib 3 rows.

Cast off in rib.

LEFT FRONT AND NECK EDGING

With right side facing and 3mm (US 2-3) circular needle, k10(12:14:16) sts across left sleeve, k last st tog with first st on safety pin of left front, k2, pick up and k90(94:98:102) sts down left front neck, then 100 sts down left front edge to cast on edge. 203(209:215:221) sts.

1st row P1, [k1, p1] to end.

2nd rib row K1, [p1, k1] to last 2 sts, p2.

These 2 rows **form** the rib.

Rep the last 2 rows twice more and the first row again.

Cast off in rib.

TO MAKE UP

Join raglan and neckband seams. Sew on pockets. Join side and sleeve seams. Sew on buttons.

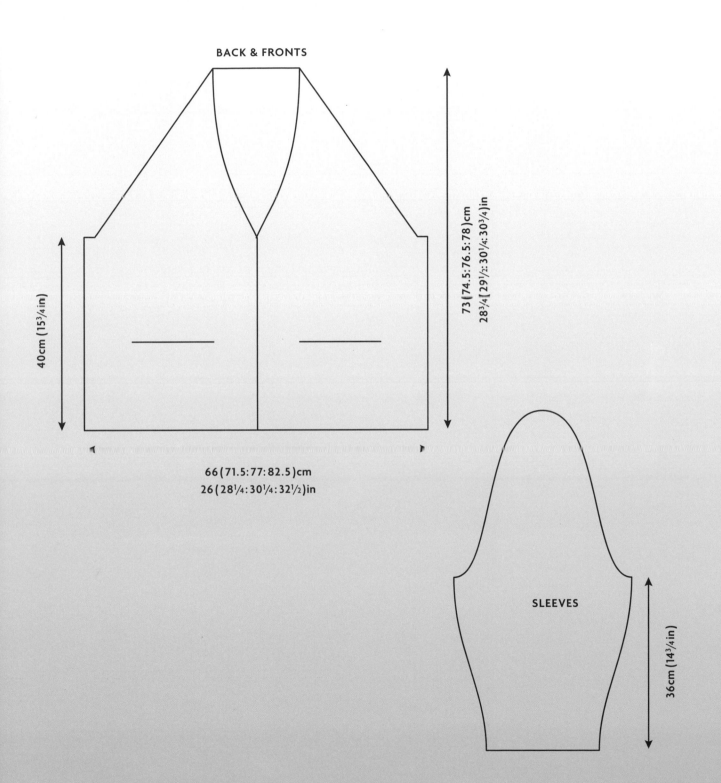

BACK & FRONTS

73 (74.5:76.5:78) cm
28³/₄ (29¹/₂: 30¹/₄: 30³/₄) in

40cm (15³/₄in)

66 (71.5:77:82.5)cm
26 (28¹/₄:30¹/₄:32¹/₂)in

SLEEVES

36cm (14³/₄in)

Hanging Pockets

If you find you are always short of storage space then this will prove the perfect method for de-cluttering your house. All that these hanging pockets need is a hook, so they can be placed on the back of a door or even on a wall. These are made using a double knitting-weight cotton yarn, that will ensure a durable, sturdy knit that is perfect at keeping its shape even when it is holding objects of varying sizes and weights.

SIZE

Approximately 31 x 66cm (12¼ x 26in)

MATERIALS

* 5 x 50g balls of Debbie Bliss Cotton DK in mink (A) and one ball in each of duck egg (B) and avocado (C)
* Pair each of 3.75mm (US 5) and 4mm (US 6) knitting needles
* 36 x 71cm (14¼ x 28in) piece of fabric
* 31 x 66cm (12¼ x 26in) piece of pelmet weight buckram
* Sewing thread
* 43cm (17in) length of wooden dowel to fit through the hanging loops

TENSION

20 sts and 28 rows to 10cm (4in) square over st st using 4mm (US 6) needles.

ABBREVIATIONS

See page 11.

TO MAKE

Lower pocket

** With 3.75mm (US 5) needles and A, cast on 63 sts.

Moss st row K1, [p1, k1] to end.

Rep this row 3 times more.

Change to 4mm (US 6) needles and work in patt as follows:

1st patt row (right side) [K1, p1] twice, k to last 4 sts, [p1, k1] twice.

2nd patt row K1, p1, k1, p to last 3 sts, k1, p1, k1.

These 2 rows **form** the main patt and are repeated.

Patt 2 rows.

Dec row [K1, p1] twice, ssk, k to last 6 sts, k2tog, [p1, k1] twice. 61 sts.

Beg with a 2nd row, work 13 rows in patt.

Dec row [K1, p1] twice, ssk, k to last 6 sts, k2tog, [p1, k1] twice. 59 sts.

Beg with a 2nd row, work 21 rows in patt.

Work 4 rows in moss st. **

Foldline row (right side) P to end.

Backing

*** Next row K1, p1, k1, p to last 3 sts, k1, p1, k1.

Next row [K1, p1] twice, k to last 4 sts, [p1, k1] twice.

Rep the last 2 rows until piece measures 65cm (25½in) from ***, ending with a wrong side row.

Now work 4 rows in moss st across all sts, so ending with a wrong side row.

Hanging loops

Next row Moss st 13 sts, * cast off next 10 sts in moss st, with one st on needle after cast off, moss st the next 12 sts; rep from * once more.

Working on the last group of 13 sts and leaving rem 2 groups of sts on the needle, moss st 27 rows, then cast off these 13 sts in moss st.

**** With wrong side facing, rejoin yarn to next group of 13 sts, work 27 rows in moss st, then cast off in moss st.

Rep from **** for last group of 13 sts.

MIDDLE POCKET

Work as Lower Pocket from ** to **, using B.

Cast off in moss st.

TOP POCKET

Work as Lower Pocket from ** to **, using C.

Cast off in moss st.

TO MAKE UP

Fold lower pocket onto right side of backing, along foldline. Join pocket to backing along side edges. Arrange middle and top pockets evenly spaced on the backing and join pocket sides and lower edge to backing, making sure that the cast on edge forms the top edge of the pockets. Fold each hanging loop in half and sew the cast off edge to the wrong side of the moss st top edge.

TO FINISH

With sewing thread, hand stitch vertical lines through the backing and pockets to divide in sections. Lay the fabric onto the buckram, then fold and tape the excess onto the wrong side. Topstitch around the outside edge to keep the fabric in place. Handsew the knitted piece to the covered buckram around the edges.

Indulge

Beaded Cushion

This stunning beaded cushion is pure indulgence. Perfect for adding a little luxury to every sofa and bed, this cushion cannot fail to impress. I have knitted this in a charming shade of pale lilac and have decorated it in complementary colours with delicate ribbon and a complex bead detail. Although this may appear a slightly daunting knit, it is in fact made in manageable stages, and the ribbon and bead elements are only stitched at the end once the knitting of the cushion is complete.

SIZE
Approximately 30 x 40cm (12 x 16in)

MATERIALS
* 4 x 50g balls of Debbie Bliss Baby Cashmerino in pale lilac
* Pair of 3.25mm (US 3) knitting needles
* Approximately 25g small glass embroidery beads – glass beads, size SB07 colour 8 (www.creativebeadcraft.co.uk)
* 33cm (13in) lengths of assorted widths of ribbon – we used 7mm (¼in), 15mm (⅝in) and 2cm (¾in) wide ribbons
* Sewing threads to match ribbons and sewing needle
* 30 x 40cm (12 x 16in) cushion pad

TENSION
25 sts and 34 rows to 10cm (4in) square over st st using 3.25mm (US 3) needles.

ABBREVIATIONS
See page 11.

NOTE
* The cover is worked in one piece from the back opening, across the front and ending with the flap that will tuck in.
* If you use ribbons of varying widths placed differently, you will need to adjust the instructions, but your cover front must be the same length as the back.
* When working st st channels between ridge rows, you need to work 3 rows for 7mm (¼in) ribbon, 6 rows for 15mm (⅝in) ribbon and 8 rows for 2cm (¾in) ribbon.

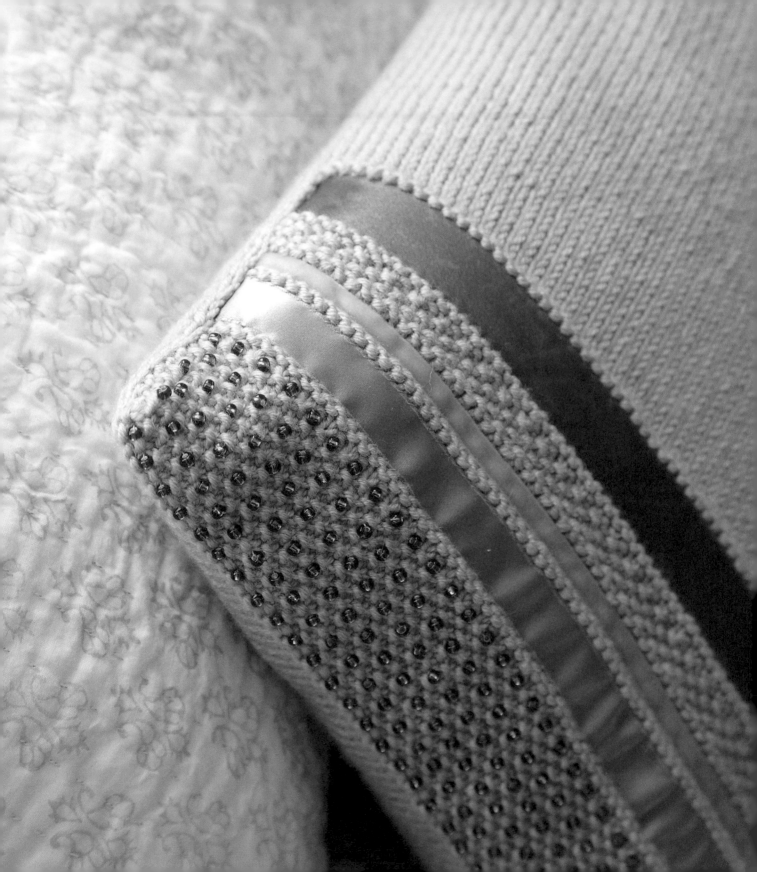

TO MAKE

The cover is worked in one piece.

Back

With 3.25mm (US 3) needles, cast on 77 sts.

Moss st row K1, [p1, k1] to end.

Rep this row 7 times more.

Beg with a k row, work in st st until piece measures 40cm (15¾in) from cast on edge, ending with a k row.

Foldline row (wrong side) K to end.

Front

Work 17 rows in moss st.

Ridge row (wrong side) K to end.

Beg with a k row, work 6 rows in st st, so ending with a p row.

Ridge row (right side) P to end.

Beg with a p row, work 3 rows in st st, so ending with a p row.

Ridge row (right side) P to end

Work 4 rows in moss st.

Ridge row (wrong side) K to end.

Beg with a k row, work 8 rows in st st, so ending with a p row.

Ridge row (right side) P to end.

Beg with a p row, work in st st until piece measures 29cm (11½in) from foldline row, ending with a k row.

Ridge row (wrong side) K to end.

Work 4 rows in moss st.

Ridge row (right side) P to end.

Beg with a p row, work 3 rows in st st, so ending with a p row.

Ridge row (right side) P to end.

Beg with a p row, work 6 rows in st st, so ending with a k row.

Ridge row (wrong side) K to end.

Beg with a k row, work 8 rows in st st, so ending with a p row.

Ridge row (right side) P to end.

Work in moss st until front measures 40cm (15¾in) from foldline, ending with a k row.

Ridge row (wrong side) K to end.

Flap

Next row (right side) [K1, p1] 3 times, k to last 6 sts, [p1, k1] 3 times.

Next row K1, [p1, k1] twice, p to last 5 sts, [k1, p1] twice, k1.

Rep the last 2 rows until flap measures 12cm (4¾in) from last foldline, ending with a wrong side row.

Now work 8 rows in moss st across all sts.

Cast off in moss st.

TO DECORATE

Working on the cushion front only, sew beads to the moss st sections, sewing a bead under alternate purl stitches, making sure beads are secure, but the thread is not pulled too tightly or it will distort the finished cushion. Slipstitch the ribbons in place to the st st channels. Fold cover along the first foldline (between the back and front) and sew side seams from fold to cast on edge (start of flap). Insert cushion pad and tuck in flap.

Watchstraps

Here is a way of brightening your wardrobe with a minimum amount of effort. Ideal for beginners, these are simple and fun knitting projects that can be made in a variety of colour combinations and to your personal specifications. Each watchstrap requires only a small amount of yarn, so they are perfect for using up the remnants of assorted colours that are undoubtably hanging around the bottom of your knitting bag.

SIZE
Moss stitch strap
Approximately 1.5 x 51cm (⁵⁄₈ x 20in)
Garter stitch strap
Approximately 2 x 50cm (³⁄₄ x 19³⁄₄in)

MATERIALS
Moss stitch strap
✷ 1 x 50g ball of Debbie Bliss Eco Baby in blush (A)
✷ Pair of 3mm (US 2-3) knitting needles
Garter stitch strap
✷ 1 x 50g ball of Debbie Bliss Eco Baby in each of three colours – mint green or mauve (B), ecru (C) and rose or blush (D)
✷ Pair of 3mm (US 2-3) knitting needles

TENSIONS
27 sts and 50 rows over moss st and 26 sts and 45 rows over garter st, both to 10cm (4in) square using 3mm (US 2-3) needles.

ABBREVIATIONS
See page 11.

MOSS ST STRAP

With 3mm (US 2-3) needles, using the thumb cast-on method and A, cast on 139 sts.
Moss st row K1, [p1, k1] to end.
Rep this row 3 times more.
Cast off in moss st.

GARTER STITCH STRAP

With 3mm (US 2-3) needles, using the thumb cast-on method and B, cast on 130 sts and k 2 rows.
K 2 rows in C.
K 2 rows in D.
K 2 rows in C.
K 2 rows in B.
Cast off with B.

TO FINISH

Darn in yarn ends. Attach watch to strap and tie around wrist.

Shrug

This delicate, show-stopping long line shrug in a gorgeous shade of pastel pink is one of the prettiest items in this book. Perfectly suited to be worn at home or to a party, this shrug looks stunning when paired with a graceful floaty dress. The shape of the shrug, with its simple lines and rolled edges, is soft and flattering on your body, whilst the fabric created by the beautiful mohair yarn is light and supple, ensuring the outfit underneath is partially revealed rather than drowned in weighty wool.

MEASUREMENTS

To fit bust

81–86	92–97	102–107	112–117	122–127	cm
32–34	36–38	40–42	44–46	48–50	in

Finished measurements

Cuff to cuff

124	130	136	142	148	cm
48³⁄₄	51	53¹⁄₂	56	58¹⁄₄	in

Length to shoulder

75	76.5	78	79	80.5	cm
29¹⁄₂	30¹⁄₄	30³⁄₄	31	31³⁄₄	in

MATERIALS

* 6 (7: 8: 8: 9) x 25g balls of Debbie Bliss Party Angel in rose
* One long 4mm (US 6) circular knitting needle

TENSION

22 sts and 30 rows to 10cm (4in) square over st st using 4mm (US 6) needles.

ABBREVIATIONS

See page 11.

BACK

With 4mm (US 6) circular needle, cast on 88 (98:108:118:128) sts.

Beg with a k row, work in st st backwards and forwards in rows throughout.

Work 12 rows.

Inc row K4, m1, k to last 4 sts, m1, k4.

Work 3 rows.

Rep the last 4 rows 28 times more. **146 (156:166:176:186) sts.**

Shape sleeve

Cast on 2 sts at beg of next 44 (46:48:50:52) rows. **234 (248:262:276:290) sts.**

Work 36 (38:40:42:44) rows straight.

Shape upper arm

Cast off 7 sts at beg of next 10 rows and 7 (8:9:10:11) sts at beg of next 8 rows. **108 (114:120:126:132) sts.**

Shape shoulder

Cast off 14 (15:16:17:18) sts at beg of next 4 rows. **52 (54:56:58:60) sts.**

K 1 row.

Cast off.

LEFT FRONT

With 4mm (US 6) circular needle, cast on 15 (21:27:33:39) sts.

Beg with a k row, work in st st backwards and forwards in rows throughout.

Work 2 rows.

Shape front edge

Next row K to last st, m1, k1.

Next row P to end.

Rep the last 2 rows 4 times more. **20 (26:32:38:44) sts.**

Inc row K4, m1, k to last st, m1, k1.

Next row P to end.

Next row K to last st, m1, k1.

Next row P to end.

Rep the last 4 rows 11 times more. **56 (62:68:74:80) sts.**

This completes the front edge shaping

Inc row K4, m1, k to end.

Work 3 rows.

Rep the last 4 rows 16 times more. **73 (79:85:91:97) sts.**

Shape sleeve

Next row Cast on 2 sts, k to end.

Next row P to end.

Rep the last 2 rows 21 (22:23:24:25) times more. **117 (125:133:141:149) sts.**

Work 36 (38:40:42:44) rows straight.

Shape upper arm

Cast off 7 sts at beg of next row and 4 foll right side rows, then 7 (8:9:10:11) sts at beg of 4 foll right side rows. **54 (58:62:66:70) sts.**

Shape shoulder

Next row P1, [p2tog] 26 (28:30:32:34) times, p1. **28 (30:32:34:36) sts.**

Next row Cast off 14 (15:16:17:18) sts, k to end.

Next row P to end.

Cast off rem 14 (15:16:17:18) sts.

RIGHT FRONT

With 4mm (US 6) circular needle, cast on 15 (21:27:33:39) sts.
Beg with a k row, work in st st backwards and forwards in rows throughout.

Work 2 rows.

Shape front edge

Next row K1, m1, k to end.

Next row P to end.

Rep the last 2 rows 4 times more. **20 (26:32:38:44) sts.**

Inc row K1, m1, k to last 4 sts, m1, k4.

Next row P to end.

Next row K1, m1, k to end.

Next row P to end.

Rep the last 4 rows 11 times more. **56 (62:68:74:80) sts.**
This completes the front edge shaping.

Inc row K to last 4 sts, m1, k4.

Work 3 rows.

Rep the last 4 rows 16 times more. **73 (79:85:91:97) sts.**

Shape sleeve

Next row K to end.

Next row Cast on 2 sts, p to end.

Rep the last 2 rows 21 (22:23:24:25) times more.
117 (125:133:141:149) sts.

Work 37 (39:41:43:45) rows straight.

Shape upper arm

Cast off 7 sts at beg of next row and 4 foll wrong side
rows, then 7 (8:9:10:11) sts at beg of 4 foll wrong side rows.
54 (58:62:66:70) sts.

Shape shoulder

Next row K1, [k2tog] 26 (28:30:32:34) times, k1.
28 (30:32:34:36) sts.

Next row Cast off 14 (15:16:17:18) sts, p to end.

Next row K to end.

Cast off rem 14 (15:16:17:18) sts.

CUFFS

Join upper arm and shoulder seams.

With right side facing and 4mm (US 6) needles, pick up and
k54 (57:60:63:66) sts along row-ends at end of sleeve.

K 2 rows.

Cast off.

RIGHT FRONT EDGING

With right side facing and 4mm (US 6) needles, pick up and k42
sts along shaped right front edge and 130 (134:138:142:146) sts up
front edge. **172 (176:180:184:188) sts.**

Cast off.

LEFT FRONT EDGING

With right side facing and 4mm (US 6) needles, pick up and
k130 (134:138:142:146) sts down left front edge and 42 sts along
shaped edge. **172 (176:180:184:188) sts.**

Cast off.

TO MAKE UP

Join side and underarm seams.

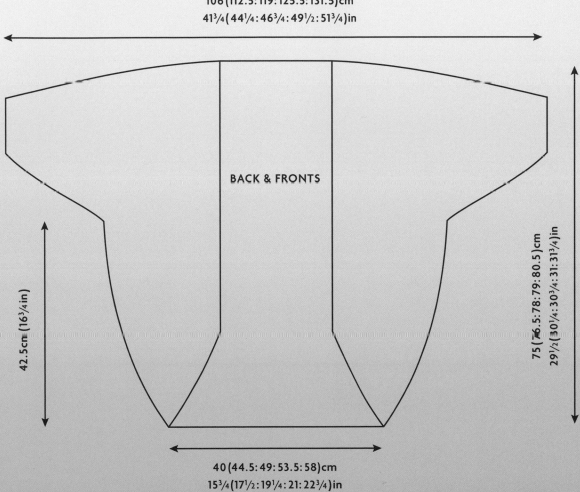

106 (112.5 : 119 : 125.5 : 131.5)cm
41³/₄ (44¹/₄ : 46³/₄ : 49¹/₂ : 51³/₄)in

BACK & FRONTS

42.5cm (16³/₄in)

75 (76.5 : 78 : 79 : 80.5)cm
29¹/₂ (30¹/₄ : 30³/₄ : 31 : 31³/₄)in

40 (44.5 : 49 : 53.5 : 58)cm
15³/₄ (17¹/₂ : 19¹/₄ : 21 : 22³/₄)in

Keepsake Box

Here is an ingenious keepsake box that is suitable for storing your most treasured items. Create a pleasing knitted fairisle background to sit within a frame to showcase all your precious family heirlooms that would otherwise be out of sight or gathering dust. This delightful project will brighten any room and can be made in a variety of colourways, whatever best suits your special keepsake. So not only will you keep your memento safe, you will also be presenting it in pride of place.

SIZE
Approximately 25 x 25cm (10 x 10in)

TENSION
28 sts and 31 rows to 10cm (4in) square over patterned st st using 3.25mm needles.

MATERIALS
✱ 2 x 50g balls of Debbie Bliss Baby Cashmerino in silver and 1 x 50g ball in each of ruby, baby pink, ecru, indigo and baby blue, plus oddments of apple
✱ Pair of 3.25mm (US 3) knitting needles
✱ Box frame – we used Ribba Frame no. 000.780.32 in white (ww.ikea.com)
✱ Decorative pine strip – available from timber merchants and DIY stores

ABBREVIATIONS
See page 11.

KEY FOR CHART OVERLEAF
☐ silver
■ ruby
☐ baby pink
☐ ecru
☐ baby blue
■ indigo
☐ apple

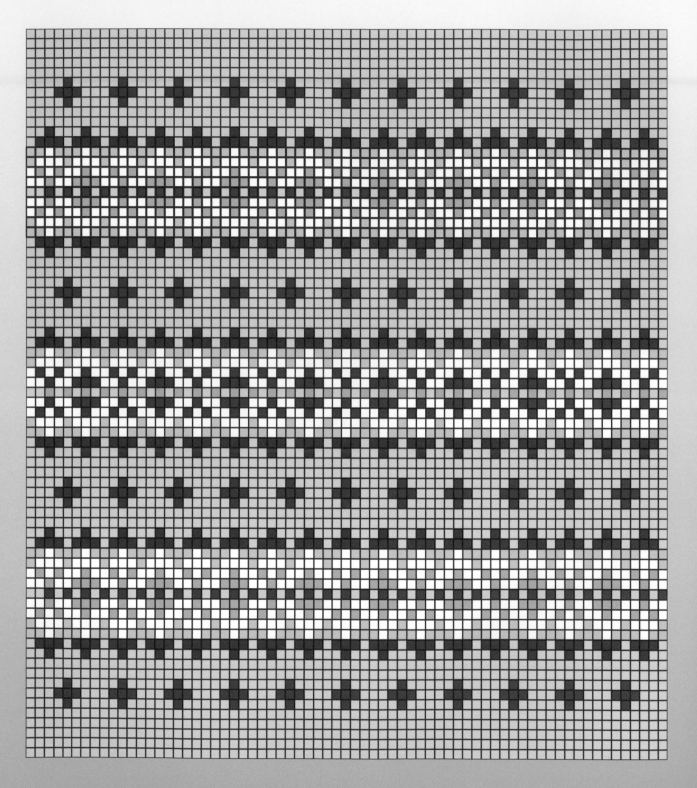

TO MAKE

With 3.25mm (US 3) needles, cast on 69 sts.

Beg with a k row, work 5 rows in st st.

Foldline row (wrong side) K to end.

Beg with a k row, work 73 rows in st st from chart, so ending with a k row.

Foldline row (wrong side) K to end.

Beg with a k row, work 5 rows in st st.

Cast off.

FRAME

Using the decorative pine strip, make a frame the same size as the box, paint the frame to your colour scheme using sample match pots. We painted ours with light grey paint, then painted over with a slightly pink off white, we then distressed the frame by lightly sandpapering the painted surfaces, to show the under paint and wood in places. We applied silver coloured metal leaf in places using gilding size.

TO COMPLETE

Remove the backboard, mount and glass from the frame. Cut a piece of mountboard or cardboard slightly smaller than the inside of the box and stretch the knitted piece over the board, folding the excess over onto the back of the board and fix in place with glue or tape, the foldline rows at the top and bottom will help. Attach your mementos to the covered board, if they are light enough, you could use the hook side of hook and loop tape, then slip inside the box. Attach the distressed frame to the box with double sided tape. If you are unable to make your own frame, Frame Factory offer a mitring and joining service. Depending on the depth of your mementos, you can either replace the glass in the frame or leave it out.

Headband

This is an exceptionally simple project to make. Knitted in two separate strips which are then joined together at the end, even the most inexperienced knitter will immediately succeed with this practical headband. As well as being a speedy knit, this headband takes only a single ball of Cashmerino Aran yarn to complete. Perfect for hours spent lounging around the house, you will find yourself wearing this cute headband morning, noon and night.

SIZE
Approximately 11cm (4¼in) wide

MATERIALS
✳ 1 x 50g ball of Debbie Bliss Cashmerino Aran in plum
✳ Pair of 4.50mm (US 7) knitting needles

TENSION
21 sts and 34 rows to 10cm (4in) square over moss st using 4.50mm (US 7) needles.

ABBREVIATIONS
See page 11.

MAIN BAND

With 4.50mm (US 7) needles, cast on 23 sts.
Moss st row K1, [p1, k1] to end.
Rep this row throughout.
Work in moss st until piece measures approximately 46cm (18in) from cast on edge.
Cast off in moss st.
Join cast on edge to cast off edge.

CENTRE BAND

With 4.50mm (US 7) needles, cast on 11 sts.
Beg with a k row, work in st st until piece measures approximately 13cm (5in) or until just enough yarn to work the cast off row remains.
Cast off.

TO FINISH

Wrap centre band around main band and join cast on edge to cast off edge. Move centre band to sit around seam of main band.

Lace Collar

One of the best ways to enliven any plain dress or blouse is by layering one of these graceful lace collars over the top. Here I have made the collar in a subtle shade of pale lilac, but if you want to make your outfit even more striking choose a bold, vibrant colour. Made from only one ball of Rialto Lace yarn, this project can be made in a relatively short amount of time. Ensured to turn heads, there is no reason why you shouldn't knit yourself one – or even two – of these.

SIZE
Approximately 10cm (4in) at widest point x 62cm (24½in) around lower edge

MATERIALS
✳ 1 x 50g ball of Debbie Bliss Rialto Lace in lilac
✳ Pair of 3.75mm (US 5) knitting needles

TENSION
28 sts and 35 rows to 10cm (4in) square over patt using 3.75mm (US 5) needles.

ABBREVIATIONS
s2togkpo slip next 2 sts together as if to k2tog, k1, pass 2 sts over.
Also see page 11.

TO MAKE

With 3.75mm (US 5) needles, cast on 175 sts.

K 1 row.

Now work in patt as follows:

1st row (right side) K3, [yf, k3, s2togkpo, k3, yf, k1] to last 2 sts, k2.

2nd and every foll wrong side row K3, p to last 3 sts, k3.

3rd row K3, [k1, yf, k2, s2togkpo, k2, yf, k2] to last 2 sts, k2.

5th row K3, [k2, yf, k1, s2togkpo, k1, yf, k3] to last 2 sts, k2.

7th row K3, [k3, yf, s2togkpo, yf, k4] to last 2 sts, k2.

8th row K3, p to last 3 sts, k3.

Rep the last 8 rows 3 times more.

Next row K3, [k3, s2togkpo, k4] to last 2 sts, k2. **141 sts.**

K 1 row.

Next row K5, [k2tog, k6] to end. **124 sts.**

Cast off knitwise.

TO FINISH

Make two twisted cords each approximately 38cm (15in) long and attach one to each end of cast off row, knotting the ends to prevent unravelling. Pin out to size and block to shape.

Chevron Cushion

Add a quirky, yet elegant touch to your room with this startling chevron cushion. This zig-zag design is a classic and is, surprisingly, easier to achieve than it looks. The design is reflected in the edging of the cushion and accented by the simple button detail. It is worth knitting this in bold and unusual colour combinations as the pattern will make more of an impact. But you can, of course, knit this in much paler shades if you desire a more subtle effect.

SIZE
Approximately 35cm (14in) square

MATERIALS
✳ 2 x 50g balls of Debbie Bliss Baby Cashmerino in sienna (M) and 1 x 50g ball in each of lilac pink (A), pale lilac (B) white (C) and peach melba (D)
✳ Pair of 3.25mm (US 3) knitting needles
✳ 7 buttons
✳ 35 x 35cm (14 x 14in) square cushion pad

TENSION
25 sts and 34 rows to 10cm (4in) square over st st using 3.25mm (US 3) needles.

ABBREVIATIONS
p2sso pass 2 slipped sts over.
Also see page 11.

TO MAKE

With 3.25mm (US 3) needles and A, cast on 101 sts.

1st (buttonhole) row (right side) K14, [yf, k2tog, k10] to last 15 sts, yf, k2tog, k13.

2nd row P to end.

Now work in patt and stripe sequence as follows:

Work 2 rows in each of B, C, M, D and A.

1st row (right side) K2, skpo, * k9, sl 2, k1, p2sso; rep from * to last 13 sts, k9, k2tog, k2. **85 sts.**

2nd row P7, * [p1, yrn, p1] in next st, p9; rep from * to last 8 sts, [p1, yrn, p1] in next st, p7. **101 sts.**

Cont in patt until work measures 30cm (12in) from cast on edge, ending with a 1st row in M. **85 sts.**

Cont in M only.

Foldline row (wrong side) K to end.

Beg with a **k row**, work a further 34cm (13½in) in st st, ending with a k row.

Foldline row (wrong side) K to end.

Beg with a **k row**, work a further 10cm (4in) in st st, ending with a k row.

K 2 rows.

Cast off.

TO MAKE UP

Fold piece along foldlines and join side seams. Insert cushion pad. Sew on buttons.

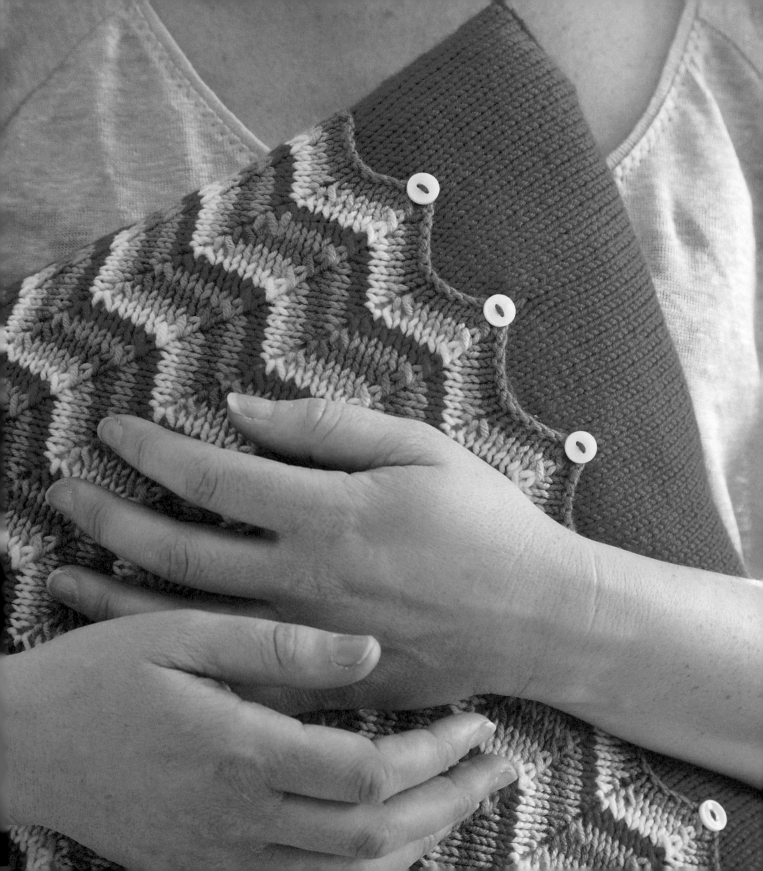

Lacy Shawl

With its gently scalloped triangular shape, this exquisite wrap shawl
sits weightlessly across the shoulders and drapes downwards to a point
at the centre back. It is the perfect showcase for the breathtakingly
beautiful fern lace stitch, which is actually deceptively easy to knit.
In this delicate lilac shade, this lacy shawl is so elegant it could be just as
easily worn for an evening social event as around the home.

SIZE
One size approximately 212cm (83½in)
wide x 112cm (44in) deep

TENSION
17 sts and 13 rows to 10cm (4in) square over
patt using 5mm (US 8) needles.

MATERIALS
* 5 x 25g balls of Debbie Bliss Angel in lilac
* One long 5mm (US 8) circular knitting
  needle
* Pair of 5mm (US 8) knitting needles

ABBREVIATIONS
sk2togpo slip 1, k2tog, pass slipped st over.
Also see page 11.

TO MAKE

With 5mm (US 8) circular needle, cast on 361 sts.

Work backwards and forwards in rows.

K 3 rows.

Now work in patt as follows:

1st row K4, skpo, k3, [sk2togpo, k3, yf, k1, yf, k3] to last 12 sts, sk2togpo, k3, k2tog, k4.

2nd, 4th, 6th and 8th rows K3, p to last 3 sts, k3.

3rd row K7, [sk2togpo, k2, yf, k3, yf, k2] to last 10 sts, sk2togpo, k7.

5th row K6, [sk2togpo, k1, yf, k5, yf, k1] to last 9 sts, sk2togpo, k6.

7th row K5, [sk2togpo, yf, k7, yf] to last 8 sts, sk2togpo, k5.

These 8 rows **form** the patt and are repeated.

Cont in patt until 21 sts rem, ending with a wrong side row and changing to 5mm (US 8) straight needles when appropriate.

Next row (right side) K4, skpo, k3, sk2togpo, k3, k2tog, k4.

2nd, 4th, 6th and 8th rows K3, p to last 3 sts, k3.

3rd row K7, sk2togpo, k7.

5th row K6, sk2togpo, k6.

7th row K5, sk2togpo, k5.

Cont in this way until 3 sts rem.

K3tog and fasten off.

154

YARN DISTRIBUTORS

For stockists of Debbie Bliss yarns
please contact:

UK & WORLDWIDE DISTRIBUTORS
Designer Yarns Ltd
Units 8-10
Newbridge Industrial Estate
Pitt Street
Keighley
West Yorkshire BD21 4PQ
UK
tel: +44 (0)1535 664222
fax: +44 (0)1535 664333
e-mail: enquiries@designeryarns.uk.com
www.designeryarns.uk.com

USA
Knitting Fever Inc.
315 Bayview Avenue
Amityville
NY 11701
USA
tel: +1 516 546 3600
fax +1 516 546 6871
www.knittingfever.com

CANADA
Diamond Yarn Ltd
155 Martin Ross Avenue
Unit 3
Toronto
Ontario M3J 2L9
Canada
tel: +1 416 736 6111
fax: +1 416 736 6112
www.diamondyarn.com

MEXICO
Estambres Crochet SA de CV
Aaron Saenz 1891-7
Col. Santa Maria
Monterrey
N.L. 64650
Mexico
tel: +52 81 8335 3870
e-mail: abremer@redmundial.com.mx

DENMARK
Fancy Knit
Storegade, 13
8500 Grenaa
Ramten
Denmark
tel: +45 86 39 88 30
fax: +45 20 46 09 06
e-mail: Kelly@fancyknitdanmark.com

FINLAND
Eiran Tukku
Mäkelänkatu 54 B
00510 Helsinki
Finland
tel: +358 50 346 0575
e-mail: maria.hellbom@eirantukku.fi

FRANCE
Plassard Diffusion
La Filature
71800 Varennes-sous-Dun
France
tel: +33 (0) 3 85282828
fax: +33 (0) 3 85282829
e-mail: info@laines-plassard.com

**GERMANY/AUSTRIA/SWITZERLAND/
BENELUX**
Designer Yarns (Deutschland) GmbH
Welserstraße 10g
D-51149 Köln
Germany
tel: +49 (0) 2203 1021910
fax: +49 (0) 2203 1023551
e-mail: info@designeryarns.de
www.designeryarns.de

ICELAND
Storkurinn ehf
Laugavegi 59
101 Reykjavík
Iceland
tel: +354 551 8258
fax: +354 562 8252
e-mail: storkurinn@simnet.is

ITALY
Lucia Fornasari
Via Cuniberti, 22
Ivrea (TO)
10015
Italy
e-mail: luciafornasae@hotmail.it
www.lavoroamaglia.it

NORWAY
Viking of Norway
Bygdaveien 63
4333 Oltedal
Norway
tel: +47 516 11 660
fax: +47 516 16 235
e-mail: post@viking-garn.no
www.viking-garn.no

SPAIN
Oyambre Needlework SL
Balmes, 200 At.4
08006 Barcelona
Spain
tel: +34 (0) 93 487 26 72
fax: +34 (0) 93 218 6694
e-mail: info@oyambreonline.com

SWEDEN
Nysta garn och textil
Hogasvagen 20
S-131 47 Nacka
Sweden
tel: +46 (0) 708 813 954
e-mail: info@nysta.se
www.nysta.se

AUSTRALIA/NEW ZEALAND
Prestige Yarns Pty Ltd
Unit 6
8-10 Pioneer Drive
Bellambi NSW 2517
Australia
tel: +61 02 4285 6669
e-mail: info@prestigeyarns.com
www.prestigeyarns.com

BRAZIL
Quatro Estacoes Com
Las Linhas e Acessorios Ltda
Av. Das Nacoes Unidas
12551-9 Andar
Cep 04578-000 Sao Paulo
Brazil
tel: +55 11 3443 7736
e-mail: cristina@4estacoeslas.com.br

HONG KONG
East Unity Company Ltd
Unit B2, 7/F Block B
Kailey Industrial Centre
12 Fung Yip Street
Chan Wan
Hong Kong
tel: (852) 2869 7110
fax: (852) 2537 6952
e-mail: eastunity@yahoo.com.hk

RUSSIA
Golden Fleece Ltd
Soloviyny proezd 16
117593 Moscow
Russian Federation
tel: +8 (903) 000-1967
e-mail: natalya@rukodelie.ru
www.rukodelie.ru

TAIWAN
U-Knit
1F, 199-1 Sec
Zhong Xiao East Road
Taipei
Taiwan
tel: + 886 2 27527557
fax: +886 2 27528556
e-mail: shuindigo@hotmail.com

THAILAND
Needle World Co Ltd
Pradit Manoontham Road
Bangkok 10310
Thailand
tel: 662 933 9167
fax: 662 933 9110
e-mail: needle-world.coltd@
googlemail.com

SOUTH KOREA
AnnKnitting
#1402 14F, Dongjin Bldg
735-6 Gyomun-dong,
Guri-si
Gyeonggi-do
471-020
South Korea
tel: +82 70 4367 2779
fax: +82 2 6937 0577
e-mail: tedd@annknitting.com
www.annknitting.com

For more information on my other books
and yarns, please visit:
www.debbieblissonline.com

Editorial Director Jane O'Shea
Creative Director Helen Lewis
Commissioning Editor Lisa Pendreigh
Editor Louise McKeever
Designers Katherine Case and Ros Holder
Photographer Penny Wincer
Stylist Mia Pejcinovic
Production Director Vincent Smith
Production Controller Aysun Hughes

Quadrille
craft

www.quadrillecraft.co.uk

First published in 2013 by
Quadrille Publishing Limited
Alhambra House
27–31 Charing Cross Road
London WC2H 0LS
www.quadrille.co.uk

British Library Cataloguing-in-Publication Data
A catalogue record for this book is available from the British Library.

ISBN 978 184949 269 0

Printed in China.

Acknowledgements

This book would not have been possible without the generous
collaboration of the following people: Rosy Tucker, who played a
huge part in producing projects and working on ideas for this book.
Jane O'Shea and Lisa Pendreigh at Quadrille Publishing who are
wonderful to work and make each book I publish with them a joy.
Katherine Case and Ros Holder for the fantastic book design. Mia
Pejcinovic, the stylist, for capturing the idea and the look of the book
perfectly. Penny Wincer for the beautiful photography. Penny Hill
for essential pattern compiling and organising knitters. The knitters
for creating perfect knits under deadline pressure: Mrs Baker, Cynthia
Brent, Pat Church, Shirley Kenneth, Maisie Lawrence, Mrs Reay, Frances
Wallace and Mrs Watson. Heather Jeeves, a fantastic agent. The
distributors, agents, retailers and knitters who support all my books
and yarns with enthusiasm and make everything I do possible.

If you have any comments
or queries regarding the
instructions in this book,
please contact us at
enquiries@quadrille.co.uk.